MASTERING ONLINE MEETINGS

52 Tips to Engage Your Audience and Get the Best Out of Your Virtual Meetings

MICHAEL FRAIDENBURG

Copyright © 2020 by Michael E. Fraidenburg
All rights reserved.
First paperback edition January 2020
Book design by Istvan Szabo, Ifj. (Fiverr / Sapphire Guardian Intl.)
Original art by Victor Manuel Nieto
Contact: vicmann1407@gmail.com
Editing by Sara Seese
Contact: saramegseese.wordpress.com

ISBN 978-1-7061-1448-2 (paperback)

Published by CCPress
www.CooperationCompany.com
www.MasteringOnlineMeetings.com

ADVANCE REVIEWS

I facilitate lots of online meetings and they can be almost impossible to do well. Michael Fraidenburg's book zeros right in on practical, useful, insightful, and creative tips that I have already begun to use to better engage participants and make productive use of everyone's time. In terms of cost-effective investment, you will recoup the purchase price in the first 5 minutes of your first meeting!

Dale Burkett
Sea Lamprey Program Director
Great Lakes Fishery Commission

As someone who facilitates online meetings at least once per month, I'm always looking for ways to increase participant engagement. This book provides a one-stop-shop for tools and techniques that spark active meeting participation.

Laura Johnson
Communications Coordinator for a State Agency

Great practical advice... As an experienced facilitator, I've struggled with the transition to increasingly using the virtual meeting space. For example, it's a challenge to keep on-line sessions focused on outcomes and participants actively engaged... Given the human resources we spend meeting on-line, the book is a great value to maximize the effectiveness of this resource.

Rich Lincoln
Founder and Senior Advisor Ocean Outcomes

You had me at tip #1! Michael Fraidenburg's book is a game changer. It is a must-read for anyone who struggles with how to run more effective online meetings or wants to run their online meetings even better.

As a consultant who spends most of my time in online meetings, I'm often frustrated with technological issues, lack of participation and follow-though, and how to get more done in less meeting (and re-meeting) time. This book is organized and written in a way that makes it easy to find topics and offers tips and resources that you can begin using immediately. I've already started using the tip on how to easily include information visually with free online tools.

Betty Lochner
CEO, Cornerstone Coaching and Training

Mastering Online Meetings takes many of the skills excellent meeting facilitators use and applies them to online meetings, which in many ways, are more challenging than in-person meetings. I've experienced a lot of awkward silences in response to questions during conference calls, so I found the prompting questions offered to deal with silence in online meetings to be especially helpful. This should be required reading for anyone who will lead online meetings.

Steve L. McMullin, Ph.D.
Past-President, American Fisheries Society

I've been helping organizations plan and design better online meetings for years, but Michael Fraidenburg's new book, *Mastering Online Meetings*, has taught me a lot. His 52 detailed tips cover pretty much every topic a planner and leader of remote meetings could ever want, from discovering the best combination of tools (many of which are free!), why you need to treat every agenda as a work plan, and dozens of tips for keeping participants actively engaged - and much more. I highly recommend this book for remote meeting newcomers and experts alike. Your meeting participants will thank you again and again.

Nancy Settle-Murphy
Guided Insights (www.guidedinsights.com)

Michael Fraidenburg's new book *Mastering Online Meetings* is excellent... Michael is a master facilitator, a remarkable teacher, and a darn good writer.

I am looking forward to sharing Michael's book with my colleagues and clients. Many organizations are committed to enhancing collaboration while also reducing their carbon footprint. So, they are dramatically increasing their use of online meetings to forego travel costs and eliminate fossil fuel consumption. *Mastering Online Meetings* will soon be a go-to design guide for successful online meetings in organizations that are committed to a more sustainable future.

Brian Stenquist
Professional Facilitator and Founder of Meeting Challenges

If you've ever been in a bad online meeting (and, let's be honest, who hasn't), this book is for you. I participate in online meetings several times a week, and most of them aren't as effective as they could be. In *Mastering Online Meetings*, Michael Fraidenburg gives 52 tips to make your online meetings as good as they can be. Some tips are strategic (use storytelling to engage the audience) and some are practical (use a really BIG screen), but all are sure to make your next online meeting better.

Ben C. West, Ph.D.
Director of Strategic Partnerships, and Professor University of Tennessee

I have struggled with how to handle many difficulties when conducting both online and in-person meetings. Michael Fraidenburg's book has a wealth of great ideas on how to deal with common and not-so-common difficulties. I plan on consulting this book often.

Dr, Scott Bonar, Professor
University of Arizona

DEDICATION

For all the people who make our communities more cooperative places to work and live by changing "I want..." into "We need..." conversations.

CONTENTS

Introduction: Getting a Grip on Your Online Meetings 11
Tools of the Trade: You're Only as Good as Your Tools 15
Before the Meeting Tips: By Failing to Plan, You Are Planning to Fail 27
During the Meeting Tips: First Rule for a Good Meeting— Engage
    Your Participants 37
Holding Their Attention: Hosting a Meeting is Easy... Holding
    Participants' Attention is Hard 45
Information Gathering Tips: Information is Uniting 59
Idea Generation Tips: Now That's a Good Idea! 69
Evaluation Tips: Evaluation is a Path to Wisdom 83
Decision Making Tips: Decide Where You Want to Go 97
After the Meeting Tips: When the Meeting is Over, It's Not Over 115
Continuous Self-Improvement: Slow Improvement is not Bad,
    Standing Still is Bad 121
Conclusion: A Person's Most Important Achievement is their Next One. 129

ACKNOWLEDGMENTS

Special thanks to my wife, Linda Fraidenburg—always willing to make room in our life for my projects, not to mention letting me bug her with logic, communication, and how-to writing questions.

Many thanks to Betty Lochner for the idea for this project and encouragement that was a gentle but resolute breeze pushing me in the right direction. *Cornerstone Coaching and Training,* http://www.cornerstone-ct.com.

INTRODUCTION:
GETTING A GRIP ON YOUR ONLINE MEETINGS

What is this book about? Let me answer that question with two questions.

- What makes online meetings more difficult than face-to-face meetings?
- Can you afford bad online meetings?

If you want people to work together, meetings are essential. That's a no-brainer. And, in this day of dispersed teams, overcrowded schedules, and high travel costs, online meetings are now essential. Unfortunately, online meetings are notoriously awful. Bad online meetings cost money and productivity. So, your choice to learn how to improve online meetings is a good investment. Here are tips to help you reduce stress and show leadership because you can make online meetings work.

There are a lot of reasons why online meetings are tough. You, as the meeting leader, cannot see the participants or, at best, only see them sitting in front of their computers.

People can tune out without being noticed... "Oh, that looks like an interesting YouTube cats-being-cute video!"

You cannot read the room for non-verbal cues that indicate if group members are confused, worried, or, simply not paying attention... "Another online meeting—great, time for a quick yoga break!"

The ever-shortening attention span of the people around us is made worse because the online meeting environment is passive, just sitting and watching a computer screen, rather than active—doing things with real people in a real meeting room... "Next time, I think I'll bring a pillow!"

An online meeting is inherently slower and less efficient than a face-to-face meeting... "Ugh! We talk a lot, but don't ever seem to decide anything!"

Finally, while the situation is improving, people are still dragging their feet to accept online meetings as "real" meetings... "I did not have time to prepare, so I'll just play it by ear, they'll never notice!"

The reality is that we are attending more online meetings every year and that trend will continue. The video conferencing market is currently predicted to grow 20% each year for the foreseeable future, according to Video Conferencing Daily, a newsletter from Logitech. While there are numerous challenges in running an effective online meeting, there are also substantial benefits.

You *do* save time, money, and reduce your carbon footprint because meeting participants do not travel.

You *do* have the chance to increase diversity because an online meeting can have a wider reach across political, cultural, economic, stakeholder, expertise, and geographic boundaries than one limited by location.

You *do* have ever-improving tools because web conferencing software is becoming more abundant, functional, and easier to use.

Introduction

Still, the obstacles to better online meetings are real. Whether collaborating through screen sharing, telephone, audio sharing, chatboxes, or other methods, successful online meetings require a conscious and deliberate application of technology and careful leadership to create meetings that work. The chief goal remains the same as for face-to-face meetings: to make good decisions and foster collaboration, not to save money. So, it is vital we learn to run good online meetings because they are here to stay. The question is, how do you make them more successful?

You will find 52 easy-to-use, no-nonsense, actionable tips to improve your online meetings. This book is different because it focuses on practical tips that address common challenges with online meetings. This is a handy guide for increasing productivity, increasing efficiency, and getting more concrete outcomes from your online meetings.

TIP of the WEEK You don't have to make a bunch of changes at once. Consider one of these three convenient ways to use these tips to build up your own and your team's skill set.

1. Pick a day each week to read a tip and implement one new skill at a time. By the end of the year, your online meetings will improve!
2. Give copies of this book to your team so everyone improves together. A standing agenda item in a weekly staff meeting can then easily become a quick discussion on how team members successfully applied the tips. Everyone's meetings will improve as a result.
3. Use this book as a problem-solving reference. Because it is organized into logical topics that mirror the challenges most of us encounter, you should be able to find the tip you need quickly and easily. Identify your problem by using the Table of Contents, then head right to a solution.

Running effective online meetings isn't simply a matter of doing the obvious things like having a good agenda and starting on time. While these are important, they are just the beginning. The key to holding effective meetings online is to organize and run them in a way that matches the capabilities of the online environment—and that environment has special strengths and weaknesses.

Now, it's time to start improving. Keep reading to get 52 tips on how to make online meetings work.

TOOLS OF THE TRADE: YOU'RE ONLY AS GOOD AS YOUR TOOLS

/Tools of the trade/ *idiom*

"a set of tools or skills that are necessary for a particular kind of job or work." (Merriam-Webster)

If you were a carpenter, would you show up at the job site with only a hammer and a saw? I hope not! However, when I help people who are new to leading online meetings, I often see this common mistake. They are slow to tool-up for the task. If you want to be a carpenter, get specialized carpenter tools; if you want to lead online meetings, get specialized tools for the job. Two common truisms that apply to trades like carpentry apply equally well to our work leading online meetings: *"the right tool for the right job,"* and *"you are only as good as your tools."*

Tip 1: Gear Up with the Right Tools of the Trade

Need: When you shop for meeting management tools, look for applications that fit your purpose and are of high quality. With the wide variety of technologies available, this can be a daunting challenge.

Solution: To avoid being overwhelmed by so many choices, progressively build up your toolkit.

Application: Look for tools to meet your present needs—one at a time. Then commit to continuously expanding and modifying your toolkit so that, over time, you end up with the best toolbox for your specific needs.

Also, change your mindset. Most people I meet who are new to online meetings think that acquiring tools is an expense. Instead, reframe your thinking to look at these as investments. Just as a master carpenter invests in a great suite of specialized tools, you should follow that role model and invest in great tools.

Next, change your boss's mindset. Often people new to online meeting management tell me that their boss hands them an assignment, the Microsoft Office Suite, and a web meeting platform, and assume that's enough. If I've just described your situation, it is time to correct that assumption. To perform the assignment of managing online meetings with excellence, you need specialized hardware (multiple monitors, robust video and sound cards, digital graphics tablet, etc.) and specialized software (mind mapping, drawing, whiteboard, survey tools, etc.). In a nutshell, if the boss asks you to lead online meetings, tell him/her that budget support is needed so you can do that job effectively; just as essential equipment would be supplied for any other project in the organization. Telling the boss that you require more money to do the assigned job can be one of those awkward moments, but you need to do it.

Tip 2: See More so You Can Do More—Use an Additional or Extra-Large Monitor

Need: The manager of an online meeting has a lot to manage at the same time. Switching between applications seamlessly can be one of the most difficult skills to master. Meetings can be interrupted, delayed, or lose continuity if the meeting manager struggles, or worse, fumbles transitions between applications.

Solution: Acquiring more screen capacity gives a meeting leader additional real estate to work with when managing online meetings. More screen capacity simplifies technology management and increases productivity. Opening and using multiple windows is a primary requirement for managing online meetings. A second monitor or a widescreen monitor that hosts multiple open windows provides the ability to prep the next one or two applications you want to use. Then, when you need to switch, simply grab the new application and slide it over to the projecting monitor, the one that is being viewed by the audience. You can also use the additional space for scratch work or to have other communication applications running—perhaps to receive input via social media (such as a monitored Twitter feed), or to help you send and receive emails and instant messages. To do this kind of simultaneous work, you need adequate real estate (monitor space).

Application: Consider shifting a variety of tasks over to the additional windows.

- Monitor incoming messages (text messages and social media) by keeping them visible in a second window.
- Just as you spread out several items on your desk to arrange them in a logical work order, with sufficient screen space you can spread

out and stage applications so they are ready to use without awkward application switching.
- While projecting a working document from the main screen you can open the original version on your second screen to have easy access for a before-and-after comparison.
- Surf the web for extra information while not disrupting the presentation being projected from the main screen.
- Take notes on the second monitor without disrupting the projection from the main monitor.
- Run a background application such as an online survey or gathering information from remote participants as they react to a speaker who is presenting on the main screen.

Reduce work, reduce confusion, and reduce stress by adding more screen real estate to your meeting manager's toolkit.

Tip 3: Meet Between Meetings—Blend Asynchronous and Synchronous Meeting Tools to Create Your Online Meeting

Need: Face-to-face meetings have plenty of pitfalls, and online meetings share most of them—plus, they add their own challenges. You'll encounter problems such as participant interactions that are too complex to manage remotely, complicated by the inability to read and manage nonverbal interactions, along with the ever-present press of too much work and not enough time.

Solution: Counter these problems by expanding your definition of what you mean by a "meeting." Include all Internet interactions that fit your purpose, including meeting opportunities between the meetings. Knowing the difference between the two terms *synchronous* and *asynchronous* will help you with this expanded mindset.

Synchronous means working together at the same time. Meeting participants log in to your online meeting software at the appointed date and time to address a common agenda simultaneously. An example is a video conference.

Asynchronous means working together but at different times. Meeting participants show up to your online meeting software on their own schedule, again to address a common agenda. An example is a blog website.

Application: Consider the differences and identify the factors you can use to select the right mix of synchronous and asynchronous tools to achieve your "meeting" agenda.

Synchronous meetings allow participants to interact with each other online, in real time. Conference calling and Internet video communication are the most common tools. Synchronous communications work well when there are a limited number of participants or a need for immediate, interactive give-and-take. Disadvantages include difficulty giving adequate time for everyone to speak, vulnerability to technology breakdowns, interruptions such as a dog barking in the background, and hassles with time-zone coordination. Synchronous tools are a good choice when immediacy is required, as in emergency decision making. They also are beneficial when a more collegial and interpersonal interaction is desired, allowing collaboration to emerge. Synchronous meetings work best if the agenda is not too large or complex.

An asynchronous meeting allows participants to interact with each other on their own schedules. Shared Internet platforms like blogs, wikis, online polling, and shared document editing are the most common tools. A participant logs in reviews input that other participants have provided, and adds to the evolving conversation by typing in their remarks. Advantages include the ability to accommodate very large audiences, elimination of time zone conflicts, prevention of disruptive interruptions, and, with the right tool, facilitation of interactions between participants because people can cross-comment on each other's input. Disadvantages include the lack of instant feedback, reduced interpersonal interaction, and the demands on participants to take additional initiative, not only to participate but also to manage the technology to join the conversation. Asynchronous tools don't work well for pressing issues but they are definitely a good choice for gathering input, implementing more formal evaluations (such as generating lists or gathering votes), and getting a large audience involved. They are also a better fit for a long or complex agenda.

When designing your meetings, decide what mix of synchronous and asynchronous tools will work best. It's not a choice between one or the other. Blend the best of both to create an online meeting that incorporates the right series of activities—in short, a meeting that fits the purpose precisely, using a combination of asynchronous and synchronous tools to address the same "meeting" agenda.

Tip 4: Group Writing—Head to Google Docs for a Free Collaboration Tool

Need: Online meetings can quickly turn into drudgery when the one-person-talking-at-a-time method is used for collecting input, especially for a dry, complex topic. Routine, unexciting subjects (such as weekly status reports) invite non-talking participants to mentally leave the meeting even though their computers are still connected.

Solution: Collect and disseminate information in a new and interactive way. Wouldn't it be useful to have several people contribute to the same document whenever you are leading an online meeting? Completing tasks like generating a list of ideas, drafting a report, planning a presentation, drafting a project plan, etc.? Well, Google makes group writing—the process of multiple participants contributing inside the same document—not only possible but easy. Meeting participants can use this tool synchronously during the meeting or asynchronously between meetings.

Application: To give you an example, I once asked meeting participants to share their personal best management practices on how to open a difficult conversation with landowners. From their hand-held devices, in the meeting room, they navigated to the document I had set up on my Google account and input their brainstorm entries. Each person's answers were added to the document *in real time* during that segment of the meeting. As the list grew, I projected it for everyone to see. The finished product is shown below. For rapid, simultaneous work on a product, add Google Docs to your toolbox.

Brainstorm Question: What are the best ways you have found to start a difficult conversation with landowners?

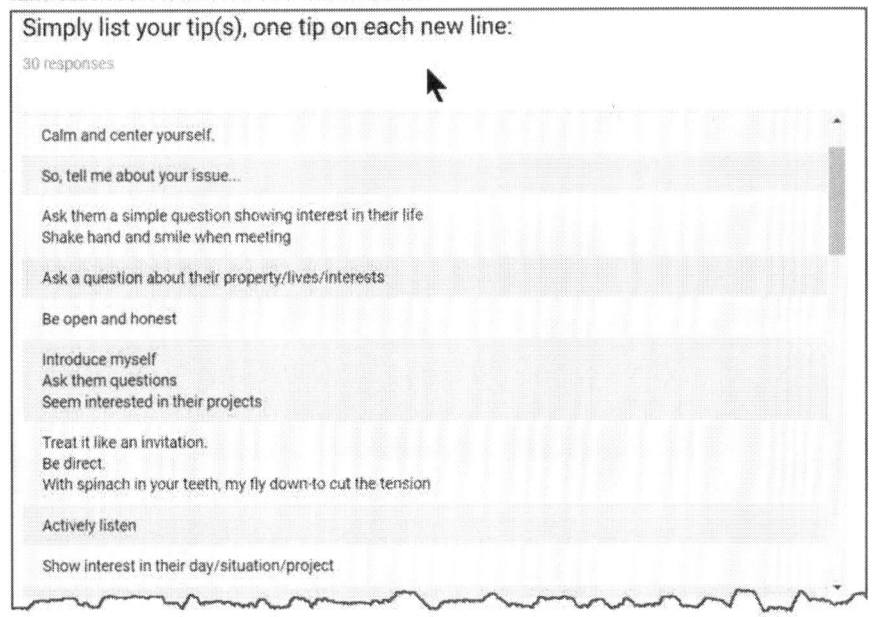

Simply list your tip(s), one tip on each new line:
30 responses
Calm and center yourself.
So, tell me about your issue...
Ask them a simple question showing interest in their life
Shake hand and smile when meeting
Ask a question about their property/lives/interests
Be open and honest
Introduce myself
Ask them questions
Seem interested in their projects
Treat it like an invitation.
Be direct.
With spinach in your teeth, my fly down-to cut the tension
Actively listen
Show interest in their day/situation/project

Tip 5: Don't Let the Good Stuff Get Away—Catch It Using a Screen Capture Tool

Need: Good things happen, on-screen, during an online meeting—but if you are not quick enough, they can get away. If your meeting is moving too fast to capture important concepts by typing out a narrative, you need a better solution.

Solution: You're probably familiar with the saying, "A picture is worth a thousand words." It's especially applicable if typing is too slow. There are a number of screen capture utilities that, essentially, take a snapshot of what appears on your computer screen. As a bonus, many of these apps provide more functionality than merely taking a picture. If you want to research the range of tools available, use a search term like, "Reviews of Screen Capture Tools." But if that is more than you want to tackle right now, there are other options.

Application: Here are four easy and effective tools you can use with no or little cost.

Windows' Snipping Tool—Free—For Still Images

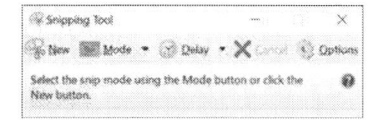

Snipping Tool is a screenshot utility included in Windows. It can take pictures of an open window, rectangular areas, a free-form area, or the entire screen. Snips can then be annotated using a mouse or a tablet, saved as a standard image file, e-mailed, or pasted into a document. To find it, enter "Snipping Tool" in the Task Bar's search box at the bottom of your screen.

macOS's Grab Tool—Free—For Still Images

This Mac screen capture tool makes it possible to take pictures (screenshots) of all or part of your screen and save them as standard image files. Just like the Windows Snipping Tool, Grab has several screen-capture modes and it also supports keyboard shortcuts. Grab comes included with all recent versions of macOS.

Jing—Free—For Still Images and Recording Videos

This always-ready program from TechSmith allows you to instantly capture images and record simple videos—then save them, paste them into a document, or share them with anyone as a standard graphics or video file. Jing is a great tool for capturing all or part of what you see on the screen during your online meetings. You can also video record mouse movements and record your voice narrative with the video. See, https://www.techsmith.com/jing-tool.html. This is the better free option. But, with Adobe's plans to retire Flash at the end of 2020, Jing's current video format .swf will no longer be supported by web browsers. As a result, TechSmith is planning to replace Jing. Go ahead and sign up for Jing now because Jing users will get email updates on progress via the email address they used when setting up their TechSmith account.

Snagit—Low Cost—For Still Images and Recording Videos

Snagit is another always-ready program from TechSmith that is similar but more powerful than Jing. This screenshot program captures still images and records a video of your actions on the screen along with audio output. Approximately $50, this software is a major bargain. Snagit provides powerful editing capability for your captured images in a nice set of utilities; my favorite is Snagit's ability to convert words in a screen capture or graphic into editable text so you can quickly paste it into another document without retyping. It is not perfectly accurate, but it is pretty darn good. And it is easy to use. Of the options presented here, this inexpensive software has the largest array of tools.

See https://www.techsmith.com/screen-capture.html.

Tip 6: Take a Note—Add a Note-Taking App to Your Toolkit

Need: Meetings usually generate collections of small bits of information, like task lists, deferred agenda items, and reminders. These can be captured in the meeting notes but retrieving and organizing these adds to the after-the-meeting workload. Even when a thought, idea, or snippet of information is written down, it needs to be easily retrievable to be valuable.

Solution: Notetaking software is like an old-fashioned 3-ring binder on steroids. To understand how a notetaking app works, recall how a 3-ring binder helps a user find the information they are looking for. A well-organized 3-ring binder uses divider tabs to separate notes into different topics. Once something has been written and stored in the binder, it is retrieved by manually flipping through the subject tabs, then searching through all the information inside that tab. Information collection is thorough, but retrieval is not exactly quick and efficient.

Notetaking applications allow *tagging* the inputted information to identify not only the subjects but also finer, more specific identifiers that are attached to each note. Notetaking apps are the digital equivalent of a 3-ring binder but, because they're digital, they make information retrieval a snap. They do more for you than even the best-organized 3-ring binder ever could.

Imagine you have a huge office with four blank walls, a ceiling, and a floor and no furniture or windows. Next, imagine that you have the world's largest supply of Post-it Notes. Then, every time you come across a useful bit of information, have an idea, or any other thought, you jot it down on a Post-it and randomly stick it anywhere inside your office. But, before you post it, you also jot down a few keywords (tags) that reference what information is on the note. Now, keep adding notes on all manner of topics until you have collected thousands of notes randomly stuck all over the walls, ceiling, and floor.

Wouldn't it be nice if there was a way to quickly sort through all the notes and retrieve only the few that you want? This capacity is what notetaking software provides. With advanced search functionality, these apps can sort through every Post-it in your imaginary office to find whatever you need in a matter of seconds. They not only search the tags, but they can search the note text itself.

The best note-taking apps let you save text, pictures, files, recorded audio, clipped pages from the Internet, and voice notes, as well as convert voice to text, extract text from graphics, and perform other functions. And, importantly for meeting managers, these apps make the same notebook available to multiple people. Note-taking apps are specifically designed for easy note taking without having to conform to a pre-determined organizational scheme, which gives you the ability to retrieve the notes in whatever way fits your needs.

Application: There are a lot of good apps for you to choose from. Wikipedia has a comprehensive review of different apps (search "note-taking software"). You will find there is a somewhat overwhelming choice. If you are new to this kind of software, consider beginning with Google Keep.

Google Keep is a notepad that connects to Google Drive and syncs across your various devices. It is free and easy to learn. Google Keep lets you take and save notes, photos, voice memos, and checklists, and then access them later on any other web-connected device. It's ideal for quick notetaking on the go. During the meeting, it is a good option for documenting lists, action items, and unanswered questions. It even extracts text that is inside a graphic and converts recorded speech into word processer text.

When you want to collaborate, you can give permission to colleagues to open and work with your notes. And you can quickly turn your notes into documents with an easy copy function to Google Docs.

It is not as robust as other note-taking apps but, all in all, it is a useful tool as well as being a good introduction to this class of software.

BEFORE THE MEETING TIPS: BY FAILING TO PLAN, YOU ARE PLANNING TO FAIL

"Success is what happens when preparation meets opportunity"
(after Seneca, 565BC and others)

We know the pain of bad meetings. The meeting with no purpose. The meeting with no advance notice or details. Or the online meeting where technological snafus get in the way. What you and your team get out of a meeting depends on what you put into meeting preparation. Meetings are intended to accomplish work. Prepare well to succeed.

Tip 7: Set Expectations—Clearly and Early

Need: Pop Quiz: Are online meetings more effective and efficient than in-person meetings?

_____ Yes   _____ No   _____ The Same

Answer: Trick question! There is a difference between the two key terms in this question. Online meetings are more *efficient* in that they save travel time and costs. And asynchronous meetings can be convenient because participants schedule their own time to attend. But online meetings are not more *effective* due to all the remote interaction and technology problems that come with them. Online meetings are inherently less productive than the same amount of time spent in an in-person meeting. What is the implication for you as the leader of an online meeting?

Solution: Set expectations with the participants and, especially, the client who is sponsoring the meeting. Give them a clear understanding that while the online meeting is convenient, they should not expect it to be as effective as an in-person meeting. If you do not spell out expectations, people will assume that you, as the meeting leader, can be as effective as you are when leading a face-to-face meeting.

Application: In the pre-meeting conversations with the meeting sponsor and participants, diplomatically reset their expectations to be in line with what you know you can realistically produce in the online meeting environment.

I have also seen a bit of over-confidence bias, especially in people new to leading online meetings. Too often these leaders think they can apply whatever works for them in their face-to-face meetings. Think again. While online meeting management tools are impressive, they don't automatically make it easier for people to work together. The online interface itself inhibits quality communication even though these tools have made it more efficient to meet online. Specialized skills and competencies are needed to lead effective online meetings; simply having the right mix of technology tools is not a guarantee of success. When managing client and participant expectations, it is better to under promise and over deliver in the first few online meetings.

Tip 8: Don't Go It Alone—at Least at First

Need: A common best management practice recommendation for online meetings is, "Know your tools, inside and out." This is necessary, but incomplete, advice. Why?

Glitches can happen even with the best systems and the most experienced meeting leaders. In an ideal world, you would be able to take your time, and learn to understand the ins and outs of the hardware, software, and connectivity options. But who among us works in an ideal world?

Perhaps the following scenario is closer to your real world: You are recruited into this leadership role because you have a reputation for being able to facilitate face-to-face meetings, then you are given an online meeting platform, then you are handed an assignment to lead a meeting to produce a result, and then told to do it in a hurry. That is a lot for one person to manage.

Solution: Recruit a tech expert onto your team. Recruit a co-facilitator at remote sites. And test the tech.

Application: Because familiarity with the normal operation of the tools doesn't guarantee a smooth experience, for at least your first few meetings recruit a knowledgeable tech-person to help you and the other members of your team. Their sole job is to deal with technical issues, help people who are having trouble logging in, field email/text questions, etc.

At remote sites where several audience members will be together in a conference room, recruit one individual who will assist you in specific ways as your co-facilitator. Ask that person to be your "eyes and ears" in the room to bring important non-verbal cues to your attention. Also ask them to handle some of the logistics at their remote site, such as queuing up questions and facilitating discussion on your behalf.

Test all of the technology in advance of the meeting's official start time. Online meeting leaders often assume everyone knows how to use the meeting technology or that it will work when it is turned on. But tech snags are common. Several five-minute tech problems add up to a major delay. Testing the technology early is a good investment to avoid wasting time or exasperating meeting participants as well as reducing your stress as the meeting leader.

It isn't a matter of whether technical problems will happen. They will. Have a Plan B or other strategy in place to avoid falling into a tech black hole that sucks the life out of your meeting.

One prevention strategy is to have everyone log on ten minutes early to ensure connecting is successful. Many platforms have a technology testing page; if remote participants have good tech support, most issues can be worked out in that ten-minute window before your meeting commences.

A second prevention strategy is to write out a step-by-step guide so participants can double-check that they know how to set up the tech at their end and easily log on to the meeting.

A third prevention strategy is to create a short (10-15 minute) pre-event. Pick a topic attractive to your audiences, like a software tutorial, a rapid-fire review of latest-events, a TED-talk presentation, or even an educational offering from a respected authority. Tech snafus are thereby confined to the pre-event time slot and will not impede the real start of your meeting.

Finally, a fourth prevention strategy (more of a backup plan) is to consider sending out copies of critical presentation materials, such as slide shows, when you send out the agenda. Then, if a technical problem crops up, you can direct participants to open these documents so they can follow along even if they can't see your screen.

Tip 9: Train First—Meet Later

Need: If your participants are new to online meeting technology or if your group needs to use sophisticated features of the technology, a lot can go wrong in a hurry just because they are not familiar with the tech system and its features. The more complex the technology, the worse this problem can become.

Solution: Make part of the group's first work be mandatory training on how to use the meeting tools. This is especially relevant for a team that will collaborate across multiple online meetings. This upfront investment of time pays big dividends because all team members can then flawlessly utilize the tech and focus on the purpose of your meetings, instead of halting progress mid-meeting to catch up those challenged by new tech.

Application: Teach meeting participants on how to use the tools.

- Host training *workshops*, especially at the start of a teamwork process.
- Run *demonstrations* using screen sharing.
- Prepare and share training *videos*.
- Provide coaching *crib notes*, including a trouble-shooting section.
- Provide detailed *checklists* giving participants cookbook instructions for the main tasks they will perform with the tools.
- Provide a *helpline* to tech support that participants can call or instant chat for problem solving.

Tip 10: Why Are We Meeting? Name the Meeting Deliverable

Need: Meetings often wander because it is not clear what the meeting is supposed to produce. Add the communication challenges of online meetings and the situation is worse. Too often, people call a meeting to discuss something without rigorously defining what that discussion is supposed to produce.

Solution: Shift thinking.

From →	"We are meeting to talk about [insert a topic or a subject]"
Shift To →	"We are meeting to create [insert the name of the meeting deliverable]."
And →	Be sure to use the specific word "deliverable" when identifying the meeting objective. Why do this? See below.

Before planning a meeting, there is a need for the organizer to clearly and precisely define the objective. The best way I've found to determine this is by having a one-on-one conversation with the meeting sponsor to obtain clarity about the concrete and tangible product needed from the meeting.

An effective meeting serves a useful purpose by producing the desired product, but you must be clear and precise about what that product is. Once the meeting deliverable is clearly defined, you can then plan the meeting and build an agenda.

If the meeting product is not known or the situation that spawned the need for the meeting is confused, build a discovery agenda to define it. The first meeting deliverable might be, "Draft a clear, actionable problem statement suitable for designing further work on this issue." Now, the purpose of the first meeting is simply to scope the problem. People can then be ready to jump in and begin productively designing a response at the next session.

Application: How do you get clear about the meeting product? Pin it down by conducting a pre-meeting intake interview with the meeting sponsor. Here are some helpful questions:

- "Why are we having this meeting?"
- "What does success mean to you?"
- "What needs to be created, decided, or agreed upon by the end of the meeting?"
- "Imagine we have a completely successful meeting. What product did we produce to make it so?"
- "Name the specific, tangible, and actionable *deliverable* you want from this meeting." In my experience, the word "deliverable" resonates with meeting sponsors for some reason. When I ask this question, I often get greater clarity of thought and the meeting sponsor can more precisely name the specific product or outcome they desire.
- "What do we need to deliver to you so you can say, 'Yes' to the course of action proposed at the end of the meeting?"
- "What document, decision, recommendation, agreement, or other product should we deliver to you when we walk out the door after the meeting?"

Be as specific as possible but try to keep it to one sentence.

Examples of Poor Objectives	Examples of Better Objectives
	Be sure to use an action verbs and tie these verbs to the nouns that name and modify the deliverables.
"Discuss stream sampling."	"Review and decide the list of standards that should go into the new stream sampling protocol."
"Progress on the new website."	"Create a prioritized list of target audiences for the new website. Assign a two-person team to recommend a mock-up of the site identifying the navigation protocol with brief notes recommending the content that should appear under each navigation link."
"Expansion of partnerships and networks."	"Outline a work plan to develop partnerships with 20 local businesses willing to host internships of our high school students."

Tip 11: Agenda—a Work Plan, Not a List of Topics

Need: An agenda is just a list of topics to be covered in a meeting, right? Not the way I see it. An agenda should be a lot more.

Solution: Reframe the purpose of the agenda by understanding these complex mathematical relationships

agenda ≠ *noun:* a list of *topics to be discussed* at a meeting

agenda = *noun:* a *work plan* to create a deliverable by the end of a meeting

I begin thinking about building a meeting *agenda* by going back in time, all the way back to the original Latin meaning of the word: "Things that ought to be done." Not "Things that ought to be talked about."

Application: As you can see, I have an opinion—an agenda is more than a list of topics. It is a work plan. Successful agendas lay out the group's sequence of meeting tasks and the series of sub-deliverables needed to create the overall meeting deliverable desired from the meeting.

Here is an example of an "Agenda as Work Plan." Read down the agenda to see the sequence of sub-deliverables that, when completed, builds to the overall deliverable for the meeting. Look also at the Process column, which is the method that will be used during the meeting to accomplish each agenda task.

Example Facilitator's Online Meeting Agenda
Meeting Deliverable: Create an initial workplan for our new strategic plan.

Topic	Product (Deliverables) from this Module	Process to be Used	Person Who Will Lead	Time
Final reminder	Recruitment	Email with time and login instructions	Mike	1:00
• Open meeting room • Assist with login issues	Resolution of tech issues	Open meeting room early, provide tech assistance as needed; open host's software apps	Mike, Jane (from IT)	1:30
Meeting Start: welcome, orientation, review meeting purpose and deliverables	• ON TIME START! • Understanding and agreement among participants	• Presentation • Questions, concerns, negotiation of changes	Mike	2:00 - 2:15
Situation assessment	List of issues that potentially needing attention in the new plan	• S.W.O.T. analysis • Joint completion of a four branched Mind Map, one branch for each quadrant of the S.W.O.T. table • Round robin reporting	Mike, John to populate Mind Map	2:15 - 3:00
Break				3:00 -
Refine situation assessment	Re-organized lists of issues	• Call-and-response discussion to winnow and organize the list of issues by categorizing, grouping, eliminating issues	Mike	3:15 - 4:15
Next meeting	• Create a list of objectives for the next meeting • Create a table of assignments and people responsible to pre-	• Negotiation by participants • Lack of dissent implies agreement	Mike	4:15 - 4:45
Adjourn				4:45

Reading down note that each module specifies how to achieve the next module on the agenda. By completing all the modules in the sequence, you achieve the deliverable for the meeting. Similarly, you can use a reverse approach to decide if you should retain or eliminate an item from the agenda. Read up the agenda and answer the question, "Why do I have this particular module on the agenda?" If you do not see a firm contribution to the module below it, that item is a good candidate for elimination.

Mastering Online Meetings

Here is how this dynamic looks:

Example Facilitator's Online Meeting Agenda
Meeting Deliverable: Create an initial workplan for our new strategic plan.

Topic	Product (Deliverables) from this Module	Process to be Used	Person Who Will Lead	Time
Final reminder	Recruitment	Email with time and login instructions	Mike	1:00
• Open meeting • Assist with ... issues	...	Open meeting room early, provide tech assistance as needed; open host's software apps	Mike, Jane (from IT)	1:30
Meeting Start: welcome, orientation, review meeting purpose and deliverables	START! understanding and agreement among participants	• Presentation • Questions, concerns, negotiation of changes • Lack of dissent implies agreement	Mike	2:00 - 2:15
Situation assessment	...of issues that potentia... ding attention in the ...	• S.W.O.T. analysis • Joint completion of a four branched Mind Map, one branch for each quadrant of the S.W.O.T. table • Round robin reporting	Mike, John to populate Mind Map	2:15 - 3:00
Break				3:00 - 3:15
Refine situation assessment	...rganized lists of issues	• Call-and-response discussion to winnow and organize the list of issues by categorizing, grouping, eliminating ...ues ... Mind Map	Mike	3:15 - 4:15
Next meeting	• Create a list ... the next meeti... • Create a table of a... and people responsible to prepare for the next meeting	...tion by participants ...of dissent implies agreement	Mike	4:15 - 4:45
Adjourn				4:45

HOW? ⬇

WHY? ⬆

DURING THE MEETING TIPS: FIRST RULE FOR A GOOD MEETING— ENGAGE YOUR PARTICIPANTS

It is hard to keep participants engaged during online meetings. Modern work lives include pressures to do more in less time and then attend more online meetings than ever before. Does the phrase "short attention span" resonate with your experiences leading online meetings? Here are ideas for keeping participants engaged and on task.

Tip 12: Communication—Make Sure It Happens

Need: An online meeting runs a higher risk of miscommunication than a face-to-face meeting does. The causes are obvious: the linear nature of the discussion and lack of non-verbal cues. For the listener, it is hard to make sure your question, "Can you tell me more about that?" remains relevant, if four people have preceded you. And it is hard for the speaker to realize their comments missed the mark if they can't see facial expressions of audience members.

Solution: Careful communication creates communicative clarity. Suffice to say, it is important to ensure that the messages being sent are received and understood as intended. When an issue crops up, pause the action and invoke active listening skills among your participants to make sure all communications are clear. Check for understanding. Especially take the time to summarize decisions; by doing so, the whole group understands that a decision has indeed been made, as well as what the content of the decision is. In an environment where someone from your meeting must justify or explain this decision to people outside of the meeting, make sure you also summarize the reasoning for the group's decision.

Application: Pick and choose from the following list to make sure the right skill is being used by the group at the right time.

Skill 1: Pay attention
"Harry, would you summarize what we just concluded?"

Skill 2: Withhold judgment
"Let's hold off evaluating things until all the information is out on the table."

Skill 3: Reflect
"Jane, would you paraphrase what we just heard?"

Skill 4: Clarify
"I am still a little confused about [insert the problem]. Please tell us more about [insert the point of confusion]."

Skill 5: Summarize
"Let me list the things we have [just learned] [decided] [etc.]."

Skill 6: Share
"Let me offer my perspective."

Skill 7: Check for understanding
"Here is what I heard, [insert summary]. Did I get that right?"

Skill 8: Check for agreement
"Do we agree that [insert summary of the agreement]? Did I get that right?"

Tip 13: Introduce Everyone to Create a Connected Group

Need: A group is not a team until they get to know one another. Team formation is a social-norming process. All the impediments of the online meeting environment hinder this norming process. In face-to-face meetings, much of this teambuilding occurs spontaneously. However, that person-to-person dynamic is weak in online meetings.

Solution: Do not presume that the people logging into your online meeting will automatically come together as a team. Create a specific process to encourage this social norming by including time and activities into meeting agendas.

Application: Consider a non-introduction introduction. You can encourage participants to connect by simply prompting small talk as people are joining the meeting. Don't miss a chance to have team members connect on a personal level and help them make their presence felt in the room. Having small talk helps people feel connected. If someone feels like they are not part of the group, they are less likely to engage and, more importantly, they won't contribute to the meeting.

If the group is new, it is good practice to have people introduce themselves. If participants are quite new to one another, include a specific module in the meeting for people to share about themselves. This can be as simple as giving their name and where they work, or as complex as asking them to share why the work you are about to do in the upcoming meeting is important to them personally.

Regardless of how deep you choose to take this getting-to-know-each-other module, be sure that you ultimately accomplish two things: first, elicit relevant biographical comments from each participant to establish their legitimacy and their credibility; and second, establish a sense of team connectedness around the common purpose for your meeting.

If your group is already close knit, then skip the formal intros or round-robin self-introductions; instead, just rattle off the attendance list so everyone knows who is online.

If the group is not yet a cohesive group, turn on the webcams. Humans are visual animals. Half of the human brain is directly or indirectly devoted to processing visual information, according to Professor Mriganka Sur of MIT's Department of Brain and Cognitive Sciences. We are exquisitely adapted to look at faces and interpret the meaning of facial expressions. And, as social animals, we are sensitive to how we are perceived by others. If people introduce themselves via a webcam, they are more likely to make a personal connection with their viewers and hold themselves accountable as team members.

If you do not have webcams available, do a picture post. A fun way to administer this is to show an assortment of pictures of the attendees.

Then, as people log in to the meeting, put a checkmark on each person's photo. Another option, if your provider lets participants write on your screen, is to have each participant write a welcome word on their own picture. This also encourages them to interact with the software at the very beginning of the meeting. As each individual introduces themselves, display their picture to everyone else using full-screen mode. To make this work, ask each participant in advance to send you a picture of themselves doing one of their favorite activities. If the situation is right and you want to do a bit of team building, ask the people to include a few remarks about what they are doing in their pictures so other meeting participants learn a little about that side of their life.

If the meeting is likely to involve dealing with disagreement, use the introduction time to enable people to talk about shared, higher purpose values for their work together. Use the professional mediator's approach: do not start the meeting asking people to talk about their positions on the divisive issue; instead, make sure that the first thing they talk about is the value they hope the group can achieve by creating a collaborative solution that benefits their community as a whole. A higher purpose is not about the details of what they want from the other parties or what they are willing to trade to get it. It reflects something more aspirational. It explains how the people involved in your meeting can make a difference by doing something that implements the values the whole group shares for the future of their community or that supports a positive relationship in the future.

A good seed question to have everyone answer in a round robin of introductions is some version of, "If we succeed in our work together, what are the benefits you hope we will create for everyone because we are working together?" Keep a mental or written list of these responses. When the meeting gets tense and disagreement starts to block progress, you can ask the group to transform their current point of disagreement into a solution that accomplishes one of these larger aspirations they said they want.

What you are doing is asking them to consider how to not let a single sticking point block progress toward a larger, more important value they hold.

Whatever you do, don't omit the simple task of writing down a log of who is present, their affiliation, and, optionally, a key point or two from their self-introduction so you have a memory prompt. If this is a formal proceeding, you need a record of attendance to document in the meeting report or minutes.

Tip 14: "Remind Me, Why Are We Meeting?" State the Objectives at the Beginning

Need: You are in a meeting where the discussion seems to be going on and on, without arriving at a conclusion. You are not sure why the meeting was called, and you are darn sure you are not the only one who is confused. Does this sound familiar? Wayward meetings have real consequences because important work goes undone. Make sure your meetings do not suffer from this problem.

Solution: This is not rocket science—make sure participants know the desired output from the meeting. And keep reminding them as the meeting progresses.

Application: At the start of a meeting, issue a reminder of the deliverable wanted from the meeting—and state this in clear, succinct, unambiguous terms. Something like the following works for me: "By the end of this meeting, we need to produce X," where X is the concrete, tangible work product (deliverable). Then answer any questions or clear up any confusion.

Keep reminding participants of this objective as the meeting progresses. If you use an online collaboration tool like a whiteboard, check to see if your software will let you put a sticker on every page with the meeting deliverable. This helps all participants be clear at all times about what the meeting is expected to produce.

To control wandering, or if there is confusion about what is supposed to happen, you can use this ever-present screen sticker to call the participants back to the meeting objective. It is simple to do. Just say, "Recall that the objective for today's meeting is [insert the deliverable]. How do we take what is happening in our meeting right now and make it address this objective?"

HOLDING THEIR ATTENTION: HOSTING A MEETING IS EASY... HOLDING PARTICIPANTS' ATTENTION IS HARD

A good meeting must first hold participants' attention. If people can stay connected with each other during an online meeting, they can create together. Unfortunately, holding attention can be a challenge. According to research by Intercall, a conference and collaboration service, conference call distractions include 65% of people doing other work, 63% sending emails, 55% eating or making food, 47% going to the restroom, and lower percentages who text, check social media, play video games, or shop online instead of paying complete attention to the conference call. Here are some ways to reduce these percentages.

Tip 15: Humans are Social Animals—Use It

Need: Just because you call a meeting and people show up at the right time and place, they are not yet a group as defined by Merriam-Webster: "A number of individuals assembled together or having some unifying relationship." They remain detached from each other until you do something to unify them into a team—a group of individuals working together to achieve a shared goal.

Solution: Capture the positive power of creating a social norm early in the meeting process. And have a way to manage the interim steps in your process to encourage collegial interaction and commitment to the shared purpose for the meeting.

Application: Be intentional as you plan.

- Ask *Expectations* questions. Have the participants discuss the expectations they have from each other to stay connected to their issue until the end. Having the group make this promise to each other is more effective than you, as the meeting leader, asking them to do it. Get the group to answer these or similar questions: "What are your expectations from one another about paying attention and avoiding distractions during our online meetings?" "What is the norm you would like to see around how we work together in these meetings?" "What are our responsibilities to one another in these meetings?" In short, devise questions to encourage the group to define their peer-to-peer behavioral expectations. Creating that social contract is more effective than you trying to impose productive behaviors.
- Plan regular interaction. Build consistent opportunities for interaction with you and among participants. Use a chat tool to encourage conversation or to have participants answer questions. For example,

you might say, "Please list and discuss with each other what are the best management practices we should use for [insert topic]?" As participants are chatting, encourage them to read and comment on each other's comments. People will tend to stay engaged because they are having a peer-to-peer conversation, which establishes an expectation to pay attention.

- Consciously create a sense of forward movement. After an interaction like the chat session above, immediately implement an interactive way to use the material created in that discussion. For example, after the first chat session, you can launch a second chat or an oral round robin asking participants to answer a follow-up question such as: "After the chat we just had, what comes next?" You can also carry the previous chat into a second, more refined chat: "Since we can't do everything you just discussed in the chat, we are starting a new chat. From all the things you just listed, which of the ideas we came up with do you think have the most promise?" This kind of second-round chatting creates forward movement on their issue. People tend to respond to an invitation to create the next thing that needs to be worked upon.
- Plan shorter segments. Because attention spans are shorter in an online meeting, these meetings need to be shorter overall and have shorter modules, more frequent breaks, a sequential organization, and a less ambitious agenda than a face-to-face meeting.

Tip 16: Keep Them Busy—Brains in Motion Tend to Remain in Motion

Need: Here is another complex mathematical formula you must master if you are going to keep online meeting participants engaged,

$$\textit{Active Brains} = \textit{Engaged Brains}$$

Attention is a limited resource. In his famous book, *Brain Rules*, John Medina presents his Rule #4: "We don't pay attention to boring things." A single activity, like passively listening during an online meeting, quickly becomes boring,

Solution: Medina recommends changing gears every ten minutes when making presentations. Otherwise, he says, people's attention will fade away. Although he doesn't say so specifically, he is probably describing face-to-face presentations. Since online meeting attention spans are shorter, I suggest this gear changing should be more frequent. Therefore, plan meetings that have a fairly rapid progression of activities. It is easier for the brain to re-engage frequently with a series of new challenges than it is to stay engaged on the same topic for a long time.

Application: Design frequent events that require active participation in your meetings. The best activities spark curiosity in your participants and make a clear, unambiguous contribution to the meeting deliverable.

- Anything that can be done *between* meetings should not be done *in* a meeting. Do that work offline (asynchronously); then bring it back as an input to the meeting or as a pre-meeting assignment to participants.
- Chunk the work into easily consumable bites. What is chunking? It is breaking down information or tasks into manageable-sized pieces. In this way, even the items that are complex can be dealt with easily, without the stress of feeling overwhelmed.
- Order these chunks in a logical sequence. It is easier to create a solution if someone arranges the work so that one item logically leads to another. This is nothing more than the basic skill of project management.

- Make each chunk as short as possible but complete enough to produce its own sub-deliverable, one that contributes to the final deliverable wanted from the meeting.
- Establish a set pattern or input model so participants know exactly how they are to contribute and when it is their turn to speak. These could be by using a round robin, separating discussions for information sharing from solution finding, or having the moderator invite each person to speak when called upon, etc.
- Give people specific tasks to do such as performing different roles during the meeting. These roles could include small group facilitators, one or more scribes appointed to capture notes and brainstormed ideas, individuals to summarize each module, etc.
- Give people alternative ways to "speak." Use the functionality of the chatbox, polls, surveys, screen sharing, whiteboards, and other tech tools. Get people to shift away from passive activities like watching and listening and encourage them to engage by clicking, writing, voting, etc.
- Capture the power of assignments and the novelty of a split meeting. If there is uncertainty surrounding your meeting issue, consider having a two-session meeting. In the morning session have the group develop a problem statement and an associated list of information needed to resolve that problem. Give assignments to be completed during the middle of the day, such as researching information or developing solution proposals. Then reconvene the meeting in the afternoon to collect the assignment results and make the decision that is needed or produce the final desired deliverable now that people had a chance to think carefully about it.

Tip 17: Make Their Brain Tingle—Use the Brain's Inherent Instinct to Seek Rewards

Need: One reason why online meetings are a challenge is because of the way our brains work. The good news is that we have powerful brains. The bad news is that we don't have long attention spans.

There is a good biological explanation. The brain evolved so we can quickly recognize and respond to sudden, dramatic changes that present survival threats. As a result, we tend not to waste our attention on safer activities like monitoring a stable environment or gradual changes that don't carry an immediate threat. So, how should we deal with this biological reality?

Solution: Research by neuroscientists Nico Bunzeck and Emrah Düzel (*Neuron*, 51-3, 2006) shows that introducing novelty captures our brain's attention. One reason why I am motivated to create meeting agendas that are "work plans"—a progressive sequence of sub-deliverables that lead to creating the overall deliverable for the meeting—is that each item in the agenda introduces a novel, next step. Without saying the words, these agendas keep asking, "What comes next?" Humans have an instinct to answer that question.

You can test this yourself. After someone delivers a status report at your next staff meeting, ask, "What comes next?" Then be silent. I predict that you will see a noticeable increase in participants' energy and focus. In online meetings, you'll make their brains tingle by engaging them with "What comes next?" invitations for forward movement.

The design principle for building an engaging online meeting is to create a long attention span by adding up a series of short attention spans (the sub-deliverables in your agenda) to finish the task (the deliverable for the whole meeting).

Application: Since frequent changes of pace and the use of attention-grabbing activities help to engage meeting participants, how often should an online meeting transition to the next action item or discussion point? Estimates of an adult's attention span range from 10 to 20 minutes. While there is no consensus for this estimate, we know attention spans are short.

We also know that people can repeatedly re-focus on a longer task. Knowing these two facts can lead to a solution by taking our cue from a university professor—John Medina, the developmental molecular biologist and author of *Brain Rules*. His students attend 50-minute-long lectures, but he organizes his presentations into 10-minute segments, using an emotional stimulus as a hook to gain attention at the start of each segment. Instead of giving one 50-minute lecture, he gives five 10-minute lectures and introduces each with an attention-getting novelty.

What is the lesson for us? Do three things: have short, frequent modules in a meeting, start each with an attention-getting device, and add interactive activities inside these shorter modules. To keep participants' minds from wandering too far, refocus with these three techniques.

Tip 18: Engage by Managing Visuals—Actively Use the Screen to Focus and Refocus Participants

Need: Vision takes precedence over the other senses. "Visual processing doesn't just assist in the perception of our world. It dominates the perception of our world" (John Medina, *Brain Rules*). If we see and hear a stimulus at the same time, we pay more attention to what is seen. And a moving object grabs our attention more than a stationary object does. This bias toward vision and motion has its roots in the fight or flight response. When we see a change in our environment, we snap to attention to figure out what is going on.

Perhaps you have attended an online meeting where a projected image stayed on the screen for three, five, or even ten minutes, without any change. Did you find yourself distracted? A lack of visual stimulus is an invitation for participants to tune out.

Solution: Give participants plenty to see on their end of the Internet connection.

Application: In online meetings, planning to change the projected image frequently is a good thing. Avoid a static image with a droning voice-over in the background. If you need to present a complex concept, build up to a complicated image in steps that tell an unfolding story.

If you are running a working meeting, build toward the solution on-screen by recording call-and-response input from participants and displaying each item as the conversation unfolds. If your software permits, have participants directly annotate the shared screen from their own computers, perhaps using simultaneous document editing or drawing on a shared whiteboard.

When you no longer need a visual, turn it off. Leaving a visual on-screen after the meeting has moved forward divides a meeting participant's attention. Do not give a participant the choice between listening to what is currently being discussed or thinking about the material still being projected on a stale slide. Since humans cannot multi-task, do not create the temptation for them to try.

In short, engage participants' brains by changing screen images frequently to support progressive refocusing on the here-and-now purpose for the meeting. And turn off stale graphics when the meeting moves on to something new.

Tip 19: Engage by Using Stories—Tell a Good Yarn and Meeting Participants Will Pay Attention

Need: You're running the meeting. You created a great agenda. You've got the facts out on the table. The need for the meeting to produce a concrete decision is undeniable.

And yet, meeting participants show only mild interest. Wandering brains and lack of commitment to the meeting's purpose get in the way of decisions and action. Whenever this happens, it's quite possible that your meeting content, while rational and logical, suffers from a lack of memorable, emotionally satisfying interactions. You spoke to your participants' logical brains but didn't connect with their hearts—their reason for acting. In turn, they never experienced that gut reaction that prompts them to say, "Yes, this is exactly what needs to happen—and now, not later. I'm ready to make a decision."

Solution: Make storytelling a regular part of your meetings. Effective storytelling activates more of the brain, puts participants in a leadership position, captures their personal motivations for doing the work, inspires action, and incorporates consequences of acting or failing to act.

Our brains are hard-wired for storytelling. Neuroscience tells us that storytelling is not something we humans just happen to do—it's part of what makes us human. Research confirms that stories speak to the two systems of our brains that, together, process information and ultimately make decisions.

The neocortex is the home of high-level thinking—logic, analysis, problem-solving, academic learning, and language. Meeting agenda items that deal with facts activate this part of the brain.

The limbic system is the home of feelings and emotions. This is where a commitment to action happens. Meeting agenda items that are about emotional impact activate this part of the brain.

Application: If your agenda objective is to initiate action, improve a group's willingness by activating both parts of their brains.

In normal life, we spin about one-hundred daydreams per waking hour. But wandering and inattentiveness drop off when we are absorbed in a good story. Humans tend to pay closer attention when they are following a storyline to its end. The story has captured their imaginations, at least for the moment. In short, humans are storytelling animals. Trigger this instinct by employing techniques such as the following:

- Asking a what-if story question: "What would be the finish to this issue if ____?"
- Setting up the problem statement for the meeting using a story that shows how the situation got to its present state: "Here is what happened that brought us to today's problem that we need to solve…"
- Asking a consequence-of-inaction question such as, "If this problem is not fixed, what would happen that we want to avoid?"
- Issuing an invitation in the meeting for forward-thinking with a question like, "How do we take this issue from where we are today and make it come out the way we want?"

And these stories do not have to be complex. A short agenda item to tell a narrative, ask participants to reflect on their own story, or describe what might happen next, can emotionally connect meeting participants to the reason the meeting product is important. If people have an emotional investment, they are more willing to act.

A good story takes listeners on a journey. A story should include specific time periods, names, and relatable characters (whoever is impacted by the group's decision). And it needs to have a beginning (set-up), a middle (contrast or conflict), and an end (resolution and key takeaways, or a question so participants must decide how they want the story to end). A story should contrast the frustrations your participants currently face with the brighter future they can create together.

I use the 6C approach as a template.

Circumstance—Set the scene of your story. Give enough background and context that participants can visualize who, where, and when. Include how the situation developed and why this topic is on today's agenda.

Curiosity—Engage participants' natural interest by describing how they are connected to the story.

Characters—Incorporate the human element by introducing who will be impacted by action or inaction from today's meeting.

Conversation—Humans are social animals and respond to a conversation far better than a list of numbers, statistics, or achievements. Avoid corporate-speak. A conversational tone forges a connection to the real people who are impacted by the impending decisions.

Conflict—The most critical part of any story is conflict, which creates a justification for the action. The main character(s) of your story must face conflict and have something significant that is at risk. This usually takes the form of a gap caused by the status quo, or an impending loss if an opportunity is not captured by a decision from this meeting.

Call to action—End the storytelling or story conversation with a description of the action or result needed from the meeting. The call to action is simply another way of naming the deliverable, the outcome you specified this meeting should produce.

Tip 20: Engage by Using Thinking Questions—When the Brain is Asked a Question, It Tries to Answer It

Need: "A growing body of literature suggests that we mind-wander, we take our mind away from the task at hand, about 50 percent of our waking moments" (Amishi Jha, Neuroscientist).

Solution: What color is your house?

After reading that question, what are you thinking about? Did you think about online meetings or did you think about the color of your house? About the painting process? About whether you need to re-paint now?

Asking a question has the interesting effect of directing, almost dictating, the next thought of each person in the meeting. This human behavior has an implication for gaining and retaining participants' attention in your online meetings. Asking a question momentarily hijacks a participant's thought process and focuses it on your question.

Humans do not consciously tell their brain to switch and start thinking about your question; it's automatic. This is the mental reflex known as *instinctive elaboration*. Multi-tasking is a myth. Neuroscience research has found that the human brain can only think about one idea at a time. So, when you ask somebody a question, you force their minds to consider only your question.

Application: Be prepared with different kinds of questions to ask so you can grab the attention of meeting participants.

Wondering questions: "I wonder what will happen if...?"

Brainstorming questions: "If we were going to... what are six ways to do it?"

Puzzle-solving questions: "How do we solve...?"

Rhetorical questions: "Let your mind wander and speculate, what if we were to...?"

Open-ended questions: "What is going on for you in this situation?"

Problem-solving questions: "Can you list the steps we should take to...?"

Now, it's your turn. I wonder what would happen if you started your next online meeting with the question, "How can we produce the deliverable for this meeting?" Then, remain silent to see what your participants come up with.

Tip 21: Use Webcams— "A Smile is the Universal Welcome" (Max Eastman)

Need: The same old problems we encountered above, inattention in online meetings and people not feeling connected to one another. If you cannot see what the other person is doing, what is to prevent them from wandering? If I cannot see your eyes, I am not sure you care.

Solution: There is nothing like eye contact to grab peoples' attention and have them make an emotional connection with one another. It is hard to check email, pet the cat, or eat breakfast during an online meeting if everyone is watching you. Watching one another establishes a social contract to pay attention and, literally, to see that everyone cares about your issue. Having participants turn on their webcams creates this kind of social contract in online meetings.

Application: Establish some simple rules for participants to use their webcams effectively.

- Turn it on. Make (at least encourage) participants turn on their webcams.
- Position. Coach participants to position the camera at or very slightly above eye level. Have them avoid using a camera angle that is lower than their eyes. We need to see their eyes front and center. If they must use the built-in camera in their computer, ask them to put the monitor on a stack of books or some other riser to elevate the camera to the best level. Participants should be able to see each other's facial expressions square on.
- Eliminate "head growths." Teach them to eliminate any object in the background that looks like it is growing from the top of their head. If I see a plant behind you that looks like it is growing from your head, that is too difficult for me to ignore. I will quit looking at your eyes and, instead, focus on your unusual head horticulture. The same is true for distractions behind you, like moving traffic. It is hard for me to ignore a moving car in the background as it goes in one side of your head and out the other. Reduce or eliminate these.
- Make "eye" contact. Let speakers know that making meaningful eye contact with the camera lens *is* making meaningful eye contact with the other meeting participants. Encourage them to look

directly into the camera lens when speaking. If that feels weird, it helps some people to imagine they can see the other participants behind the lens, as if in a face-to-face meeting. Some people find it helpful to post photos of participants behind the camera to personalize the experience. Assure them that it is okay to look away from the camera occasionally to glance at their PowerPoint slides or other items on their computer screen. Everyone in online meetings expects that; but encourage participants to look right back at the camera lens as they continue to speak, especially when delivering key points. Eye contact makes it harder for meeting participants to allow their attention to wander.

- Write it down. Take advantage of screen sharing software to visually document the meeting discussions and outcomes. Two types of brain behaviors make this an effective strategy. First, as noted earlier, is the biological imperative to follow any movement in our field of vision. If we see something moving, such as typing, drawing on the screen, or a pointer highlighting key information, we instinctively stop what we are doing to watch and assess whatever is happening. The second is a brain behavior known as *Loss Aversion Bias*. The human brain is highly sensitive to the potential of any loss. If you are documenting the outcome of a meeting, especially for important items like decisions, assignments, and negotiated agreements, people will pay closer attention because they think there is a chance they are about to miss something important. The subliminal message is, "Pay attention. If you don't, you are about to lose out on something important that will cost you in the future." That is a powerful incentive to, well, pay attention. You can make this work even better by verbally calling attention to the fact that something important is being captured on the screen at that moment.

INFORMATION GATHERING TIPS: INFORMATION IS UNITING

Good information is a basic requirement for good decisions. Without effective information gathering, it is hard for an organization to make decisions, plan for the future, and support sustained learning. When designing an online meeting, it is also important to plan how to harvest the information that is shared. Otherwise, the meeting can be unproductive. Here are some ideas for success.

Tip 22: Let Audience Size Be a Guide—Separate Working Meetings from Information Sharing Meetings

Need: A one-size-fits-all meeting format means, at best, your meeting will use the wrong process at least 50% of the time.

Solution: Make conscious choices about using different meeting designs to support different meeting purposes. Recognize that the process of sharing information and the process of using that information are separate activities. Therefore, you should separate these into different meetings.

Application: For online meetings that are intended to be "working meetings" where you hope or expect to produce a concrete, actionable deliverable, it is best to keep the number of participants small. The limitations of software make it difficult for larger groups to interact. If thirty people each speak for one minute on a single agenda item, ½ hour of meeting time has been consumed. The reality is, of course, most are really going to speak for three to five minutes each. You can manage these larger groups a bit better if your software platform supports breakout rooms, but even that is an imperfect solution. If the need for participant interaction is intense, keep the group as small as is needed for the task.

Sometimes, though, the purpose of an online meeting is to share information, such as an introduction to a new policy or procedure, or to collect simple incoming information, like group opinions, free-ranging input, or general preferences. In cases like these, a well-constructed online meeting may be an efficient way to quickly reach a lot of people. If the type of participant interaction desired is simple, the audience can be large with no adverse impact.

Tip 23: For Information Sharing, Make It Infotainment

Need: If neuroscientist Amishi Jha is right that "we mind wander... about 50 percent of our waking moments," you've got a problem if your meeting is only about delivering information.

Solution: Design the delivery of information in an entertaining way—use *infotainment*.

"*Info*" = information

"*Entertainment*" = something diverting or engaging, such as a public performance

Be engaging while being informative. Merely providing information is a fast way to lose your online audience. Create a program that captures your audience's attention *and* shares the important information you need to present.

Application: Incorporate these tips to effectively share quality content in an engaging way.

- Be prepared. Practice delivering your presentation, including using the technology, in advance of the online meeting. Make sure all of the features of the technology work. Record the practice session and watch it to learn what works and what to improve before the meeting.
- Be fast. Enough said.
- Be simple. Slides with a lot of text are confusing and hard to read. Worse, people won't remember much of what's on your slides. There is a chance, however, they will remember the conclusion your slide is presenting; therefore, build slides to reinforce your main point, not to present a lot of data.
- Continuously orient your audience. How? Use a simple headline slide that names the subject you will be exploring with the current

subset of slides. Then add that same title as a smaller headline on the remaining slides on that subject. When you move to a different subject, insert a new headline slide for that module and add that new headline to the subsequent slides in that module. This practice helps an audience focus because they have a constant reminder of why they are seeing the current slide series.

- Be a storyteller. "Let me tell you a story…". Did that pique your curiosity about what I might say next? That is why stories work. Enrich the information with stories, personal anecdotes, and/or examples that clarify and amplify the important concepts. You do not have to be a "good" storyteller. Humans are so attuned to stories that most real-world, or even imagined, stories will resonate. Try something as simple as opening your remarks with a statement that signals a story is coming next. Begin with something like, "Let me tell you about what happened when we tried _____," or "Let me tell you about the events that led to _____." Then, just be yourself and fill in the blanks in your own words. That is a perfectly fine way to use storytelling in an information-sharing meeting.

Tip 24: When Meeting to Make a Scary Decision—Use a Script that Takes Participants on a Mental Journey of Small, Incremental Steps

Need: Loss aversion was popularized by psychologists Daniel Kahneman and Amos Tversky (Science 27 September 1974). They found that humans are more likely to focus on the risk of a loss than they are to focus on a potential gain. Twice as likely, in fact. Risk perception is a way we measure fear. Risk aversion is the behavior of humans who, when exposed to uncertainty, attempt to lower that uncertainty. It is the behavior of hesitating rather than immediately agreeing to a choice with an unknown future. If that future contains the possibility of a loss or a gain, humans have a bias to make decisions to avoid a loss. The lesson for meeting managers working to get a group to make a decision is that meeting participants have a bias to avoid a loss.

Solution: Research on human decision-making behavior has shown that people are more likely to take a risk when they perceive that the current risk is similar to, but not too big a leap from, a risk they've taken previously. However, if they perceive that the risk is a large step, they are more reluctant. The implication?

Application: When you are preparing a group to make a decision, present a sequence of decisions in small, incremental chunks. Lead the meeting participants, step by step, to the final desired action. Meeting participants are more willing to consider taking a risk if they feel they are in control. If you leap to the conclusion too early, you are likely to leap past some meeting participants' willingness to take a risk.

Here is one model for processing information when the objective is to decide. Each of these four steps can be a module in your meeting agenda.

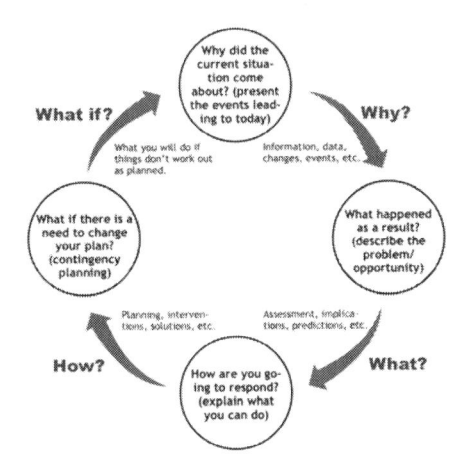

```
                    Why did the
                    current situa-
                    tion come
    What if?        about? (present      Why?
                    the events lead-
                    ing to today)

   What you will do if         Information, data,
   things don't work out       changes, events, etc.
   as planned.

  What if there is a                    What happened
  need to change                        as a result?
  your plan?                            (describe the
  (contingency                          problem/
  planning)                             opportunity)

              Planning, interven-   Assessment, implica-
              tions, solutions, etc. tions, predictions, etc.

    How?        How are you go-         What?
                ing to respond?
                (explain what
                you can do)
```

63

Tip 25: Manage the Competition from Your Screen Images—Use the "Magic B" Key

Need: If a presenter or participant in your meeting keeps talking while an old slide is still being projected, they create competition for the audience's attention. Should meeting participants pay attention to the speaker's voice or keep re-reading and considering the slide?

Solution: If a slide is no longer needed, turn it off.

Application: Simply use the "Magic B" key in PowerPoint or Keynote. Tapping the letter "B" toggles between an active and a blank screen. With nothing on the screen, the participants' attention automatically returns to what the speaker is saying. When you are ready to proceed to the next slide, toggle the screen back on by hitting "B" again. To improve an audience's focus and information retention, use the "Magic B" key to direct participants' attention by switching back-and-forth between the spoken word and the screen.

Tip 26: Information Sharing—Select Tools That Are Good for Large Meetings

Need: Imagine what it would be like to moderate a meeting where you need to collect input from one hundred people. Some meetings are simply too large to use an interactive, dialog method of information give-and-take.

Solution: When faced with the challenge of communicating with a large audience where oral dialog is not feasible, take advantage of text-based tools and features in your meeting software or available in a third-party application.

Application: Employ these simple-to-use tools to enhance your effectiveness during these large-scale meeting times.

- Hand Raise. This tool lets participants raise a virtual hand either to capture the attention of the meeting leader or in response to a question. Usually, a participant simply clicks an icon to raise their hand and clicks a second time to lower it. This allows the meeting leader to ask a question and quickly get a count of the number of participants who agree. For this technique to work, you must formulate closed-ended, two-answer questions, for example, "Yes or No," and "Option A or Option B." Usually, a reset is required to lower all the hands in preparation for the next question. If the hand-raising results are not retained by the software, automatically allowing you to download them, be sure you keep a record of the results before you reset.
- Polling. The polling feature allows a meeting leader to add more complexity by using multiple-choice questions. Typically, you launch the poll during your meeting; the software tallies the responses and provides the ability to download a report after the meeting. Polling works great when you know the questions before the meeting because you can set up the polls ahead of time. However, it is difficult to be both an effective, alert meeting leader and also prepare polls in the middle of the meeting. If the ability to create polls during the meeting is needed, recruit an assistant to do this real-time work for you. Typical poll questions could be phrased, "On a scale of one to five, indicate how satisfied you are with the way things are working now," or "Which software package do you recommend we purchase, Option A, B, C, D, or E?"

For this technique to work, the range of answers still needs to be a "closed set," that is, questions that must be answered within a range of specified options. Even if someone does not like any of the answer choices, they don't get to choose to submit their own, though you could provide the option of "None of the above."

- Narrative Survey. A narrative survey allows you to ask open-ended questions, which require a participant to write or type a response. These answers could be a list, a phrase, a few sentences, or something longer. Use this tool when you are looking for more depth or a complex response. This technique is also good when you are uncertain what the answers should be, so you are in a discovery process to figure that out. Open-ended questions with written responses can help you find out more about a situation that is not yet well understood. Here are some example questions: "How will your program implement today's decision?" "What is the quickest way to get the word out to your members about the new policy?" "What do you think the causes are?" "What, precisely, is the problem we are facing?" Check to see if your meeting management software supports narrative answers. If it does not, bring in a third-party survey or collaboration tool such as Google Docs that does support this function. Be aware of limitations; if there are multi-cultural language issues in your audience, or there is a risk of disrespect and verbal fighting among participants, be careful with this tool.

- Chat/Messaging. Most meeting platforms have a chat/messaging function. Clever use of this tool can turn it into a version of a hand raise, poll, or a mini-narrative survey. How? Think about what you could ask your meeting participants if you began your question with the phrase, "Type into the chatbox _____." You can ask them to type "Yes" or "No" (hand raising). They can type a poll-style choice, "I like Option _____." You can even encourage them to type in answers to complex questions like, "What is your assessment of the situation we are facing?" (narrative survey).

- Private Messaging. If you have confidential or contentious material that needs to be reviewed or a participant who is reluctant to speak or write in front of others, this is an option; however, it's not truly a good option. Because meetings are about collegial and transparent exchanges, retreating to private messaging blocks that value. Private messaging also is risky. It only works if the sender clicks a toolbar function to set the message as private. If the sender misses that click, everyone will get the message. A better solution is to develop ground rules which create a safe meeting environment for all participants (for example: show respect to one another, tolerate disagreement agreeably, no personal attacks permitted). If that is insufficient, take the problem offline and into a venue like a private phone call or one-on-one meeting.

IDEA GENERATION TIPS:
NOW THAT'S A GOOD IDEA!

A meeting that is not good at generating ideas is not a good meeting. Successful organizations today cope with an accelerating pace of change. More than ever, an organization will have difficulty if it cannot develop new ideas at least as fast as the world around it changes. Where do your organization's good ideas come from? While the actual answer is undoubtedly "Many places," I'll bet you are frequently asked to attend meetings in order to "come up with some ideas."

Meetings are routinely used as idea factories. Without good ideas, change doesn't happen, and progress is not made. So, what are some ways to help online meetings be more effective at generating ideas?

Tip 27: Improve Online Brainstorming—Write a Right and Tight Seed Question

Need: Innovations are vital, but often hard to develop. Unexpected problems may crop up that need immediate solutions. Sometimes an organization slips into a rut and can't get out without strong, directed efforts. The problems—the needs—are real.

But just imagine what you would do as the leader of an online meeting if you asked participants for their ideas to resolve one of these pressing issues, and everyone started talking at once! In this type of situation, the burst of creativity that brainstorming provides easily degrades into a talk-not-listen session.

Solution: Begin corralling the chaos into a more systematic information harvesting process by writing a tight seed question. If any facilitation technique has stood the test of time, it is brainstorming—but the ideas generated are only as good as the question that stimulates them. To support creativity, problem solving, or rut avoidance, identify goals for the session and *then* invite brainstorming by crafting the right and tight seed question.

Application: Brainstorming is a viable strategy in an online meeting—but it is easier to lose control in the virtual-meeting-room environment than in a face-to-face setting. When you start with a wide-open brainstorm question, you invite a free-for-all. Once an online meeting begins to get out of control, it becomes difficult to re-direct everyone back to collaborative interaction. It's better to sacrifice a bit of brainstorming *creativity* to gain more brainstorming *productivity* on a specific question. A right and tight seed question sets out both the desired outcome expected from the brainstorm session ("We need to create a list of great ideas for _____") and the sideboards that participants will use to self-select answers that are more germane ("But our answers need to stay inside the constraints of _____").

If participants are unaware of the desired end product or the constraints that must be kept in mind, brainstorming can stray far from the desired scope of the problem. First, pin these two factors down; then, begin to brainstorm. If the problem is that the group does not know what the problem really is, then ask a clarifying question like, "What is the problem we are encountering with _____, under the circumstances we have experienced of _____?" Now the vague call for "ideas" becomes a tightly-worded seed question, sparking a productive brainstorm that clarifies uncertainty. That brainstorming question shifts the group into a discovery process instead of a solution-finding process.

Tip 28: Improve Online Brainstorming—Give Them a Target

Need: Creative idea generation is often thought to be a natural process, one that just automatically happens if you ask for a brainstorm. But research indicates that in freewheeling brainstorming a group can wander and get confused about what they are being asked to produce.

Solution: It is more effective to give the brainstorming participants a specific, difficult target for the number of ideas to be generated during the brainstorming session. People do well and seem to rise to the challenge when given a specific target to hit.

Application: For you, as the meeting leader, it is nothing more complex than changing your invitation to brainstorm from, "Let's brainstorm ideas on _____." to "Let's brainstorm 12 ideas about how to deal with _____."

My usual approach is to start with a freewheeling brainstorm; then, when the idea generation slows down, I ask participants to give me X more ideas before we quit. Why this works can only be speculated, but some researchers suggest that assigning difficult goals works because individuals set a higher personal expectation for themselves. In short, set a target for participants to hit, such as, "I would like each of you to come up with your _x_ best ideas to address [seed question]."

Tip 29: Improve Online Brainstorming—Make Participants Work Alone, At First

Need: It is a popular notion that brainstorming is best when it is a completely freewheeling process to generate the maximum number of ideas. Research suggests there is a better way, at least if you factor in the desire to focus on the highest-quality ideas.

The most significant problems with a freewheeling brainstorm are production blocking and scope limiting.

Production blocking occurs because certain individuals, after generating a few initial ideas, get stuck waiting for other people to report and don't concentrate on creating additional ideas. These participants stop thinking and start waiting for their turn.

With scope limiting the thinking of meeting participants is conditioned by the ideas presented earlier in the meeting. Participants start self-censoring their thinking because prior ideas have narrowed the topic, or because one prominent idea (or strong personality) captures the attention of the group. As a result, their thinking time is spent responding to that single but forceful point of input, rather than considering a broader scope of ideas.

Solution: If the objective is to create the highest number of quality ideas, the research indicates that having individuals brainstorm on their own at first produces four times as many high-quality ideas compared with freewheeling brainstorming. (https://onlinelibrary.wiley.com/doi/abs/10.1002/ejsp.2420030402).

Application: Use silent writing to begin. After assigning the seed question, give participants a period of "quiet time." During this interval, they work on their own, without discussion, to develop an initial list of ideas. This quiet time allows participants to analyze their own thinking, combine strong points from several of their ideas, delete poor quality ideas, and revise their thinking to formulate a list of higher quality ideas. When you establish the silent writing time, be sure to promise participants that presenting their ideas will happen during a separate step which will come after the silent writing. Say something like, "You will share your ideas after your personal brainstorm, so pick your best ideas to present."

This silent writing process, in effect, sets up the first quality control filter in the idea generation process. When the silent writing is over, invite participants to share their ideas, one at a time, and hold discussion until after all the ideas are presented. If you use oral reporting to collect each participant's ideas, ask them to share brief remarks as you project their completed list to the group.

One enhancement is to provide a digital writing space to collect ideas. Have individuals type their ideas into a shared document, the chatbox, whiteboard, or equivalent visual tool that is shared with everyone. This should streamline record keeping.

Tip 30: Improve Online Brainstorming – Use Speedy Brainstorming, Especially for Group Coaching

Need: From time to time, do you find it helpful to talk with a colleague about a challenge so they can suggest solutions you haven't been able to come up with yourself? You are in good company. We all do!

Solution: Change that dynamic to one where you present your problem once, and many colleagues respond by offering their suggestions! This many-to-one coaching brainstorm is well suited for online meetings. And it allows very quick development of a lot of ideas to help solve very specific problems.

Application: Use a simple process to direct and shape this type of brainstorm event.

1. *Problem Statement.* The team member with the challenge presents a problem statement to the group. This statement should be a concise description of the issue or the condition that needs attention. It identifies the gap between the current status (situation assessment) and the desired end state (objective). The statement should focus on facts— try to address the 5 Ws (who, what, where, when, and why). Avoid conclusions, speculations, or hypotheses. Avoid asking if a solution they have in mind is a "good" one. That is a different kind of evaluation. Speedy brainstorming is only about generating ideas. The objective for this initial statement is to communicate the problem, whatever understanding exists about the causes, and the desired end state being sought. The person with the problem is defining the gap that needs to be closed, not asking for feedback on solutions they already have in mind.
2. *Clarifying Questions.* The team members ask the presenter clarifying questions—simple questions that establish or verify facts. These initial inquiries seek to eliminate ambiguity, confusion, or misunderstanding, not open new topics. Clarifying questions should not go beyond the boundaries of the presenter's problem statement. Clarifying questions have brief, factual answers. And they do not offer solutions. Confine this exploration to clarifying what the presenter said. Do not add to what the presenter said. And do not propose a solution. Examples of clarifying questions: "How much time does the project take?" "How were the students

grouped?" "What resources were used during the project?" An example of an out-of-bounds question is, "Have you thought about [insert a solution statement]?"
3. *Idea Generation.* After the clarifying questions are answered, team members type their ideas for the presenter into the meeting software (using the chatbox feature or shared document, sending a text, or writing a quick email). Do this without discussion. This is just a data dump for the person with the problem to use later.
4. *Discussion.* It is best to hold off discussing the results. Allow the presenter to digest the ideas and consider how they might use or modify them to address their areas of concern. If you feel you need or want discussion, share all the ideas with the whole group first, and then create a separate meeting module to discuss the brainstorm results.

Tip 31: Pre-decide How You Will Collect the Input from Meeting Participants

Need: It is relatively easy to generate a lot of information at a meeting. Efficiently harvesting that information so it can be effectively used after the meeting is much more difficult.

Solution: Explicitly design how you are going to capture that information well before the meeting starts, so you have it ready for immediate use after the meeting.

Application: Choose the right mix of methods; do not rely on just one option.

Oral reports. If you are asking for oral reports, you might consider a round robin with uninterrupted time for each person to present. If you cringed when I suggested that, calculating how much time that process would take, you are right. In a twelve-person meeting, if each person only speaks for five minutes, your meeting will consume an hour.

Now, make a prediction for me. If each online presenter in this 12-person meeting has only five minutes "airtime," what will they be doing during their 55 minutes of downtime? They are supposed to be listening to the other participants, but will they? Probably not. Multi-tasking, like checking email, Internet surfing, or writing the next report that is coming due, is just too tempting.

Group Writing. Set up a shared document on Google Drive or another service, and assign different sections of that document to the various participants. As your meeting progresses the participants can work on their assigned sections, perhaps taking detailed notes, or generating ideas. Before wrap-up, have folks edit each other's work. It is usually best to limit this editing to commenting or suggesting changes. Avoid large-scale changes to the original text or finicky wordsmithing—instead, assign these as after-meeting tasks.

Chat. Most web-meeting software apps have integrated chat functions. Pose specific questions or requests for feedback, then have each meeting participant enter their input into the chatbox simultaneously. If you need a summary of the findings from this input, assign one or two "reporters" to monitor the responses and give brief oral remarks at the end. Their assignment is to identify the input and the implications of that input that most impressed them. Capture these summaries in writing—they are the first draft of the group's conclusions from the meeting.

Asynchronous Input. There are many information collection tools you can use as a companion to your online meeting software (such as blogs, wikis, and worksheets). Make these available for participants to use and follow up this asynchronous collection of information with an assignment for meeting participants to review each other's input before the next in-person, online meeting. You can also ask a small team to summarize this information for the next meeting. This team's assignment is to identify the most important conclusions and the lessons they learned from their colleagues' input. Tell this team they will be given the opportunity to report at the next online meeting. Then, in the online meeting, do oral reports, group writing, or chatting to harvest the full group's reactions to the team's summary. Again, capture these comments and reactions in writing as the first draft of the completion report from the meeting.

Tip 32: Mind Mapping—Your Online Flip Chart

Need: Imagine all the ways you use a flip chart in a face-to-face meeting—including simple recording, combining similar ideas onto separate sheets, voting, even organizing input by moving paper sheets to various places on the walls. You need that capability in an online meeting as well, but you do not have a flip chart. What can you do?

Solution: Use a projected mind map. A mind map is a type of diagram that collects ideas and then organizes that information into logical categories. Lucky for us, it also works well as an online replacement for the trusty flip chart routinely used in face-to-face meetings.

Mind mapping is a highly effective tool to get information out of the brains of the people in your online meeting and to organize it logically. It, literally, becomes a map of the meaning of their ideas.

One great thing about mind mapping is that you can write down ideas in any order, as soon as they spring up in a meeting. That is a big help in online meetings; it not only preserves the advantage of free-flowing brainstorming, it also becomes an evolving organization of ideas into a relationship diagram because meeting participants also organize their ideas as they generate them. Mind mapping is a great substitute for a flip chart when you need to collect and organize ideas so that they make sense.

Application: Tony Buzan, inventor of the mind mapping methodology, suggests a step-by-step process. Here is my adaption of his advice for creating a map.

1. *Focus the Mind Map.* Write a clear, concise subject statement, such as a deliverable, seed question, topic, problem, or opportunity statement.
2. *Create a Central Node.* Place that subject statement in the center of a blank page—the Central Node. By starting with that subject statement in the center, you provide a stimulus for creativity. As participants generate ideas, they perceive they have freedom for their concepts and suggestions to spread out in all directions. An abundance of ideas then evolves naturally. Another advantage is that this central subject also can be used as a call-back to refocus a discussion that starts to wander.
3. *Add First-Level Nodes.* These are comments from participants giving additional insight and specifically addressing the need expressed in the Central Node. First-Level Nodes are connected to the Central Node with lines to demonstrate there is a logical connection between them. Your software will automatically draw these lines for you.
4. *Add Second-Level Nodes.* This information clarifies or describes what needs to be done to achieve the desire expressed in a First-Level Node.
5. *Add More Subordinate Nodes.* Add more details, if necessary, in order to explain ways to achieve the Second-Level Nodes. Be aware that your map can get confusing if you build it out beyond three levels, so consider carefully before adding a lot of detail. If the subject demands this greater level of complexity, be sure to plan how you will manage the display so participants can keep up.
6. *Use the "Notes" Function.* Most mind mapping software packages provide the ability to add a note that is specifically linked to a particular node. The note feature is usually accessed by opening a small text box that allows you to type in this additional information. The note can be toggled "open" or "closed" so it is only

Idea Generation Tips

visible on the screen when you need it. This is such a handy feature that I recommend you avoid purchasing software that does not have this capability.

To illustrate how these interconnected nodes work in a mind map, let's plan a picnic!

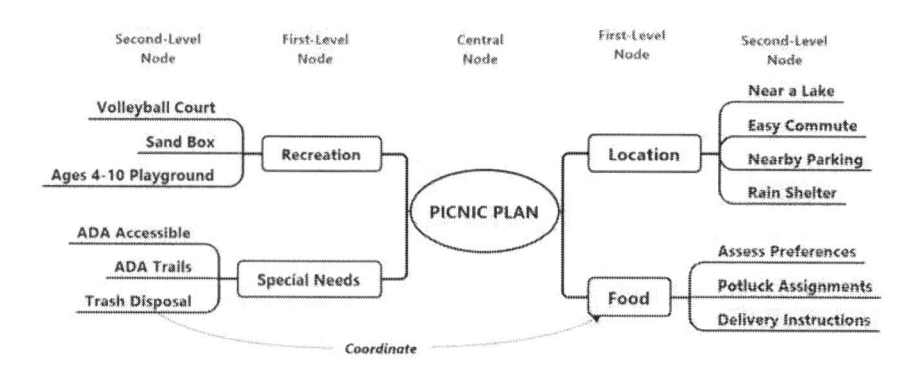

```
Second-Level      First-Level      Central         First-Level      Second-Level
   Node              Node            Node              Node             Node
                                                                   Near a Lake
  Volleyball Court                                                 Easy Commute
    Sand Box       Recreation                       Location      Nearby Parking
Ages 4-10 Playground                                               Rain Shelter
                                  PICNIC PLAN
  ADA Accessible                                                   Assess Preferences
    ADA Trails    Special Needs                       Food         Potluck Assignments
  Trash Disposal                                                   Delivery Instructions
                                  Coordinate
```

If you ask a group to brainstorm how to plan a picnic, they might easily generate ideas for location, food, special needs, and recreation (First-Level nodes). Further brainstorming should then identify what needs to happen for success with these First-Level nodes. Add these additional details into the chart as Second-Level Nodes. For example, under "Food," the group brainstorm determines that the required activities are (a) to assess preferences, (b) make potluck assignments, and (c) specify delivery instructions.

Most mind mapping software programs also support easy exporting of reports as a graphic, an ordered list, outline, word processing document, etc. A simple Internet search for "mind mapping software" will return many results which include both free and paid apps. Before you invest in a purchase, you may want to test-drive free options such as downloadable *Freeplane*, available from www.freeplane.org, or web-based www.wisemapping.com.

Tip 33: Google Docs for Brainstorming

Need: Your organization has a problem. Fortunately, you have access to some of the most creative minds in your organization, but they work at dozens of locations around the world, and there just isn't time or money to bring everyone together for a face-to-face meeting. Additionally, you know that a simple teleconference will not meet the need effectively. Your biggest concerns are the short deadline, the distance separating your meeting participants, and the complexity of the task because any of these could easily block progress. You are somewhat familiar with web collaboration tools but have no idea how to begin planning an online brainstorming session that will address all of the challenges and requirements. Lucky for you, there's a free tool that you can use!

Solution: Use Google Docs, which is a free, web-based application for creating and editing documents that are stored online. Files can be accessed from any device with an Internet connection and a suitable web browser.

How can Google Docs help with online brainstorming? This app allows multiple authors to contribute to the same document at the same time. Users can see each other's changes as soon as they are made and add notes about what others have written. With the chat function, meeting participants can have side-bar conversations with other people while they're in the document. When the brainstorm is complete, exporting the completed document to other common formats is a simple process.

Application: How can you master this technology? There are many excellent, free tutorials on how to use Google Docs that are, not surprisingly, easy to find by searching for, "How to use Google Docs." One of my favorite authors of video tutorials is Anson Alexander of www.ansonalex.com. Note: we are not affiliated in any way, I just like his tutorials.

How do you manage the brainstorming process itself? That's easy. Conduct the brainstorming session using these steps:

1. Post a blank document on Google Docs. This becomes the OFC (online flip chart) for this brainstorming session.
2. Write a tight seed question for the brainstorm. Enter it at the top of the OFC to feature it prominently where all participants can see it easily.
3. Make sure everyone can access the OFC. Either use their email addresses to permit each user to edit the shared document, or share a link provided by Google which gives the same type of permission.
4. A few minutes before the meeting starts, send each participant a reminder encouraging them to open the OFC. Include the link and any other log-in details you have set up.
5. When the meeting begins, introduce the brainstorm, coach participants so they know how to enter their ideas, and then turn them loose to enter their suggestions from their own devices. Remind them that they can use the notes function to comment on one another's entries, as well as the chat function, which allows them to talk over an idea with a colleague privately, as the brainstorming session progresses.
6. If your meeting participants are new to this technology, be prepared to meet the need for some tech support to help the people who are struggling. If you foresee that you might be busy managing other aspects of the meeting, arrange for another person to provide tech assistance. You can also create a pre-meeting tutorial and a practice document to help orient meeting participants.
7. Moderate a debrief. Reserve a little time at the end for concluding remarks or whatever conversation is needed to bring closure to the brainstorming discussion.

8. Ask one or two people to be "reporters." Instead of participating in the brainstorm, they read the other participants' comments as they are being typed into the OFC and make summary notes on what they learned from the brainstorm that they believe are most relevant to the seed question. Then have these people speak first during the debrief. Get a copy of their notes and capture these oral summaries as they are delivered because they can form the first draft of your meeting report.

9. Create a short how-to video tutorial for the participants, demonstrating the technology and introducing the brainstorming activity. Send it to participants several days before the meeting. If at all possible, make it mandatory, forcing people to view the tutorial and practice ahead of the real meeting. Post a practice OFC and have the participants go through the process to access that document and enter mock comments. That way they'll work out many of their own technology problems before the meeting even begins.

EVALUATION TIPS: EVALUATION IS A PATH TO WISDOM

The process of evaluation analyzes choices in order to decide what to do or to settle on a conclusion. During a meeting, this activity usually involves some way to systematically collect participants' opinions about the merits of the various alternatives. It serves a due-diligence purpose because it ensures the group's judgments are sound and justifiable. Use evaluation as part of an online meeting to clarify choices, focus attention on what's most important, support ongoing learning, and guide actions and decisions. If you want to improve decision making in an online meeting, improve evaluations.

Tip 34: Use a 'Secret' Facebook Group for a Quick, Easy, and Private Discussion Group

Need: Getting a group to do a thorough evaluation often requires having a difficult conversation. The quality of a difficult conversation is only as good as the comfort level people have when sharing their thoughts. It is harder to have a difficult conversation if people are aware that potential critics are listening. Make it easy for participants to openly share by constraining the initial conversation to include only the meeting participants. Providing that measure of safety can free up participants to speak (or type) what's on their minds. When they aren't worried about freely sharing their ideas, they can concentrate on tackling the difficult problem they are facing.

Solution: Sometimes it is best to hold a meeting *before* the meeting.

Yes, that's right. Choosing to have a pre-meeting discussion among your participants can work in your favor, giving them an opportunity to evaluate the problem, evaluate solution options, or evaluate different scenarios without a looming deadline. By doing this in advance, the limited time in the real meeting can now be used exclusively for closure work, such as decision making, negotiations, and consensus building.

From the convenience of their own offices (or favorite coffee shop), your meeting participants can engage in a pre-meeting discussion geared toward effective evaluation.

Application: The challenge, as always, is finding a helpful methodology or strategy. There are many online discussion forums available, but these often have steep learning curves. A good alternative is to host a "secret" (private) Facebook group. Since Facebook has over two billion users on a monthly basis, most people are already comfortable with the platform. Even if they are not familiar with it, they can learn to use it easily. And it

Evaluation Tips

supports nested commenting, which means people can reply directly to each other; a handy feature which keeps material on the same subject clustered together. While private Facebook groups are confidential, there is a caveat: if you work in the government sector, using this tool probably does not exempt you from open-government laws, so do check with your legal staff first.

You may wonder how to establish such a group. Well, building and maintaining a private Facebook Group for your meeting participants is comprised of four major elements.

1. Create an Exclusive Facebook Group. Private Facebook groups are private for a reason—not everyone can join. The administrator must approve a member's request to join. Facebook offers two options for creating exclusivity in your group: **Closed** groups and **Secret** groups. Pick the **Secret** option—it is the most private. Secret groups are not searchable via Facebook, and only people who have been approved can join. In contrast, Closed groups are publicly viewable. They can show up on newsfeeds, and the title, description, and member list are visible to anyone. Avoid this option because it is searchable on Facebook even though a viewer cannot comment.

2. Establish Guidelines for the Secret Facebook Group. It's important to give your group direction regarding the types of input that will be expected during the life of the group. As in any meeting, set ground rules. Establish clearly that the group is a safe space for people to ask questions and state opinions, no personal attacks will be tolerated, stick to the subject, respect confidentiality, and any other boundaries or parameters that you feel need to be set. Never forget that if you work in the public sector, the conversation is probably discoverable under public disclosure laws. Again, check with your legal staff.

3. Moderate Your Facebook Group. Even after starting this kind of Facebook discussion group, it will still take work to keep the discussion on-topic and moving forward. Utilize the same best-management practices that you would use in a face-to-face meeting. Begin by defining a tight seed question to keep the participants focused on the discussion. Then monitor the conversation—encourage commenting, re-direct wandering, provide summary statements once agreement and consensus emerge within the comment thread, and decide when to close the discussion on the current seed question so you can move forward to a new seed question for the next round of discussion. Don't make the mistake of planting a seed question and simply expecting the conversation to take on a life of its own. Active and frequent moderating is vital to maintaining a healthy online discussion group.
4. Maintain Group Connections. As the moderator, you need to ensure that three types of connections are forged: connect people with all pertinent content, connect people to each other, and connect people with the deliverable you expect the discussion to generate.

The stronger you make these connections, the more beneficial the group interactions will become for your meeting process—and thus the organization. With active management, a group usually meshes together and becomes a team—a great team—which is aligned around a common purpose and accomplishes great work!

Tip 35: Rank (Prioritize) a List of Items Using Polling Tools

Need: Generating ideas is easy. Ranking them is not. However, setting priorities is an important element of the work done during a meeting. It is especially hard in an online meeting to "read the group" to determine which ideas they actually prefer. Sometimes there are too many ideas for a group to manage. At other times, strong conflicting opinions arise about which ideas are most important. Having too many participants may make it difficult to negotiate a completely satisfying compromise. Perhaps the group gets into a stuck state where they cannot decide because "everything is important." Or, even employing the best plans and strategies, there simply may not be enough time left in the meeting to completely talk through a solution.

Solution: Use polling—frequently. As you design your next online meeting, consider how you normally ask questions in a face-to-face meeting. Then translate those questioning techniques into the online meeting environment by creating polls. As participants reflect, share, and compare, they become more deeply engaged with the content. By introducing a poll, you give them another reason to fully participate and make progress with the required decision. People engage when they sense forward movement toward closure.

Application: Study up on polling tools that work for your type of meeting, including the following list. Be aware that this type of tool does not have to be complex to be effective.

Round Robin Voice Input. This method works best if the group is small, if the answer is simply "Yes" or "No," or if participants will pick a single choice from a list that you provide. You can use a simple prompt: "When I call on you, name the option you think is the best."

Raise Hand. Most online meeting platforms have this feature, which is a good choice for quick comparisons. You can prompt participants to respond by saying, "How many like option 1 best? Click the 'Raise Hand' feature if you do," or "If you're ready to move to the next agenda item, click the 'Raise Hand' feature."

Google Polling. Use Google's free polling feature. Search, "Google forms."

Third-Party, Real-Time Paid Service. Many similar services exist which enable participants to complete a survey while the meeting is in progress and the software will compile the results right away. Find them with an Internet search for "online polling software." Common platforms with free introductory plans plus paid premium features include Survey-Monkey, Doodle, Poll Everywhere, and easypolls. A free, live-voting tool that might work for you is DirectPoll.

Tip 36: Use Pros and Cons Listing

Need: You've started with a right and tight seed question. You've held an excellent brainstorming session that generated several solid ideas, and everyone's agreed they're ready to move forward with the discussion. So far so good, right?

But now, when there is more than one viable option on the table, uncertainty about the merits of the choices can stall progress. After-meeting implementation can flop if participants have different understandings about why the group settled on a particular choice, especially if there was insufficient time to obtain commitments and buy-in from everyone involved. Decisions can be influenced by strong personalities whose personal bias skews the discussion in a particular direction. Emotions and reactions get in the way of clear thinking. The good news is that there is a simple solution for all of these problems.

Solution: By listing the pros (advantages) and cons (disadvantages) of each choice, the decision-making process becomes less subjective, less steered by bias or influenced by emotions, and the responses to the decision are more stable after the meeting.

Application: Pros are the arguments *for* choosing a course of action. **Cons** are arguments *against*. Once your group develops lists detailing both the Pros and Cons for each option, they can make a more informed decision.

When would you use a Pros/Cons list? Because of its simplicity, a Pros/Cons list is suitable for any situation when there is a need to compare two or more options. The decision might be as simple as whether to do something now or hold off, or it might be a more complex choice between different options. Regardless of how many choices you have, the process is the same: create a separate Pros/Cons list for each option and compare the results. If it's a single yes or no choice, the Pros/Cons list helps you evaluate where your idea is weak and strong. With that list in hand, you can identify mitigations for the key weaknesses and plan how to take advantage of the strengths. If there are several options to choose from, a Pros/Cons list will help you objectively identify the best choice.

Template for Pros/Cons Listing	
Pros	**Cons**
The Positive Aspects and Outcomes of an Option, Decision or Course of Action	Negative Aspects and Outcomes of an Option, Decision or Course of Action
Potential seed questions to ask: • What are the upsides (benefits) of this idea/option? • What are the reasons why this is a good idea? • What positive outcomes do we expect? • How will this contribute to our success? • What are the strengths of this idea/option?	Potential seed questions to ask: • What are the downsides (costs) of this idea/option? • What are the reasons why this idea presents risk? • What negative outcomes and challenges do we expect? • How would this impede or impact on our success? • What are the weaknesses of this idea/option?
Bullet List of Pros • • • etc.	Bullet List of Cons • • • etc.

How can you create a Pros/Cons list for use during an online meeting? You have two choices.

1. *Moderated Call-and-Response Facilitation.* Project the table of pros and cons using whatever software you prefer to use—although sharing your screen while using your favorite word processing software is probably all you need. Explain the process of listing the Pros and Cons to your participants. Then have each of them orally report their observations while you or an assistant type the comments into the projected document. This way, everyone can see the evolving results. However, if your group is very large or there is conflict, this may not be an effective method.

2. *Self-Catered, Free-Form Listing by Participants.* There are many real-time collaboration tools on the Internet that allow remote meeting participants to enter information into a shared document. These tools offer two key advantages: first, the participants themselves do the data entry, and second, these Internet-hosted documents update in real-time while the participants are typing their input. Everyone can immediately watch the accumulation of information from their colleagues. While a simple Internet search for a term like "online brainstorming tools" will return a lot of hits, selecting a tool does not have to be complex or take a long time. In fact, there are two simple, free solutions.

    a. *Chatbox.* Most online meeting software platforms have a **"chat"** function so remote participants can type in short phrases. One method is to use Pros/Cons as tags; meeting participants begin each of their chat comments by typing a tag, either the word "Pro" or the word "Con." Later, compile the results in an organized table or set of bullet points like the example displayed above, using the tags for identification. Another methodology separates the lists into two separate chats, one for Pros and the other for the Cons.

b. Use a shared-document service like Google Drive to post a blank Pros/Cons table. During the meeting, participants simply type their input into the correct cell in the shared document. With Google Drive, you can use "Google Doc" to "create a table" in a new document template, or use Google Sheets to create a new spreadsheet template. You can even use these tools asynchronously by having participants enter the requested information into the shared template on their own schedule. However, the asynchronous option carries the risk that the busy people you work with may not show the necessary initiative to participate. You may need to prompt people several times to complete this type of assignment.

Tip 37: Freewriting on a Virtual Whiteboard

Need: Creating a visual image of the meeting deliverable, such as a map, workflow, or process diagram, is easy in a face-to-face meeting. You just ask everyone to stand near the whiteboard, and they'll start drawing, erasing, and re-drawing the graphic until the image is refined. Kinesthetic activities such as writing and drawing stimulate creative thinking and problem solving and promote knowledge retention. They engage the brain in ways that typing and texting do not.

In an online meeting, providing opportunities for this type of creative activity is not as simple—but it is still easy, thanks to a rapidly emerging array of virtual whiteboard applications.

Solution: Inviting your team to join in an online whiteboard session may be just the breakthrough you need to tap into their creativity. These virtual whiteboards give meeting participants the ability to collaborate online, without distance getting in the way of progress.

With an interactive whiteboard, you don't just share files with participants—you also share your screen, which allows remote participants to draw directly on the image. Instead of a sequential slide presentation forcing participants to watch passively, an interactive whiteboard enables meeting participants to directly engage with the information—they can annotate the slides themselves!

Application: Using a full-featured, virtual whiteboard application, participants can draw lines, create objects, fill in shapes with color, and enter captions and text. Although each program may have unique features, an online whiteboard usually allows you to upload many types of files (drawings, maps, graphics, photos, documents, even audio and video) to share during a meeting. These shared files are then available for anyone to annotate and draw upon. Some online whiteboard apps allow sidebar chatting with colleagues via text or video feed. The most-advanced services will create a comprehensive meeting report for you by providing a means to export screenshots as each drawing develops. A few will even create a video/audio recording of the whiteboard session.

Imagine that you need to create a geographic depiction of important information. Just as in a face-to-face meeting, where the participants stand close together and draw on a whiteboard with dry erase markers, online participants can log into a virtual whiteboard and annotate the empty canvas with their input. They may add connecting lines to show relationships between objects or make secondary comments about the whiteboard picture right from their own remote office or hand-held device.

Take a look at this example, in which participants drew their weather forecast directly on top of a map of the USA. Collaborative drawing software makes it easy!

Evaluation Tips

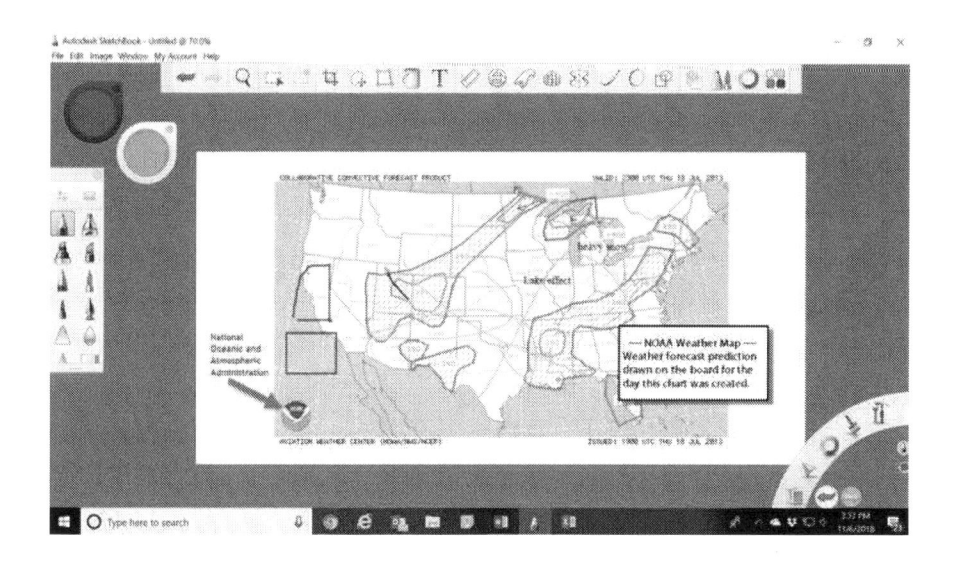

Tip 38: The 2x2 Matrix – A Simple Evaluation Tool to Get Your Whole Team on the Same Page

Need: So far, your meeting has been successful because the participants have defined several feasible solutions to a problem they face. Now the group needs to evaluate those solutions and choose the best option. For example, a group that is behind schedule needs to decide between asking to extend the product's delivery time versus meeting the deadline by sacrificing product quality. Which of these two options is better?

Getting a group of people to evaluate effectively isn't as daunting a challenge as it may seem. The objective of problem-solving meetings is to find the optimal solution, or at least to reach the best compromise that the group or organization is willing to support. That's where a 2x2 Matrix can help.

Solution: Strong opinions about the best choice often vary among individuals, making buy-in more challenging. And most meeting decisions are reviewed and approved by other people after the meeting adjourns. The 2x2 Matrix can help because it provides a number of benefits:

- ensures that multiple perspectives are considered
- improves communication among meeting participants
- creates a neutral framework, reducing the risk of bulldozing by strong-willed participants
- allows potential positive and negative consequences both to be considered prior to decision making
- helps communicate the reasons behind the final decision to stakeholders who were not in the meeting (like the boss)

Application: Be visual! Set up a blank matrix in your meeting platform software before the meeting begins.

A 2x2 matrix consists of four *meaningful* quadrants. If the quadrants do not separate opinions clearly, then it is probable that the variables you placed on the two axes of the matrix are not independent of each other.

Focus each 2×2 matrix on just one seed question. It can be tempting to try to save time by combining needs or solutions into a single diagram, but doing so typically leads to generalized discussions rather than to a focused decision.

Specify axis variables that clearly identify and separate the options being compared. Popular 2x2 matrix axis labels are Cost versus Value, Importance versus Urgency, Time versus Cost, Effort versus Impact, and Current Performance versus Needed Impact. The 2x2 matrix format is also used for exercises that collect input in four distinct categories, the most famous of which is SWOT Analysis (Strengths, Weaknesses, Opportunities, and Threats).

Internet meeting technology does not yet provide an easy way to post a matrix that allows all of your meeting participants to collaborate on the same matrix. Consider making your own solution in either group whiteboard software or a four-quadrant spreadsheet in a shared writing space like Google Sheets.

There are two ways you can have participants fill out a matrix.

1. Score all the options in the same matrix. Give each option a unique *tag*, such as A, B, and C, and ask meeting participants to place each of their tags where they think they belong, assigning value scores along the axes. A tight cluster of tags in the matrix indicates an emerging consensus about the merits of that option. If the scores are widely scattered, then there is disagreement or confusion about that option.
2. Score each option on a separate matrix. This is a good solution if you have many options because too much information in a single chart becomes confusing. Create a separate matrix for each option, and give a unique number or letter code to each *person* in the meeting. Have participants indicate their scores on the various matrices by placing their code at the appropriate place in the matrix. Then, compare results by comparing the matrices. Because each participant uses their unique identifier, you have the option of asking individuals to discuss the reasoning behind their scores.

The 2x2 matrix helps because items are scored using two independent criteria. Each axis represents a separate decision criterion. For example, here is a matrix that uses the Quality versus Delay dilemma mentioned above. In this case, the group's evaluation identifies that they believe Option C provides the best balance between these tradeoffs.

Mastering Online Meetings

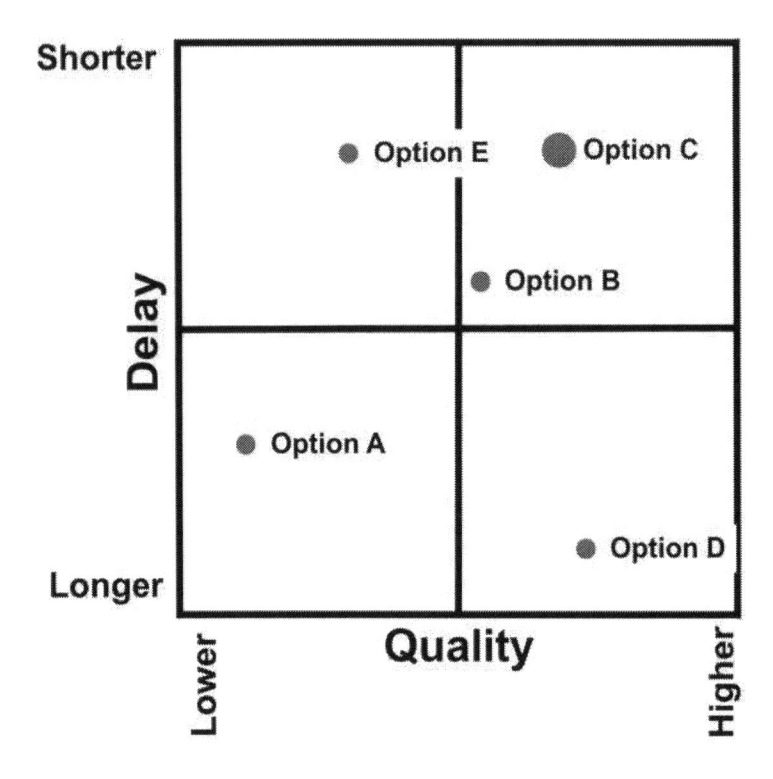

```
Shorter
       │         │
       │ ● Option E  ● Option C
       │         │
       │         │ ● Option B
 Delay │─────────┼─────────
       │         │
       │ ● Option A
       │         │
       │         │ ● Option D
Longer │         │
        Lower  Quality  Higher
```

The 2x2 Matrix provides a solid foundation for decision making by breaking a problem down into manageable components and scoring by objective values that affect the decision making. At its most basic, the 2x2 Matrix deals with the key decision dilemma faced by anyone trying to determine how to allocate limited resources. It forces a constructive and thoughtful decision by considering and choosing between conflicting values. This is a winning tool that is easy for meeting participants to grasp and use.

DECISION MAKING TIPS: DECIDE WHERE YOU WANT TO GO

If the choice is not clear, you haven't truly decided.

Tip 39: Decide How the Group Will Decide

Need: The Boy Scouts of America motto "Be Prepared" is equally meaningful for meeting leaders. If you do not have a plan identifying *how* to make the final decision, you are not prepared to draw the meeting to a successful close. Don't get to the decision point of the meeting and have to make up a process on the fly.

Solution: There are two broad approaches for "deciding how to decide." One option is for you or the meeting sponsor to choose the decision-making process, without consulting the group. The other option is to have the group negotiate and agree on the decision-making method they will use. Ask yourself, what method will help get the most out of the group and leave people feeling good about the result?

Application: Be clear. Whichever approach is right for your meeting, you, as a meeting leader, must ensure that the decision rules are clear at the beginning of the meeting. Decisions that are made by fewer people (like the boss) are quick and efficient. Decisions that are made by a bigger group of people take longer but harvest more energy and commitment from the group.

Culture matters. An organization's culture often drives how decisions are made, how well decisions are accepted, and how effectively they are implemented. Know the culture of your group and adapt your decision-making method to be a good cultural fit.

"Be Prepared" by specifically selecting a method that meets the unique needs of each online meeting.

- *One Person Decides.* This is usually the person with that specific responsibility. In this case, the meeting participants work to inform that person so he/she can make a wise choice.

- *Democratic (Majority) Decision.* Every participant votes and the option with the most votes becomes the preferred choice. One variation is to have a qualified-majority decision; in this situation, the group decides—prior to voting—what percentage or threshold is required to declare the results of the vote as the group's final decision.
- *Unanimous Decision.* Everyone has to agree. This decision standard is tough to achieve.
- *Compromise.* The group members make offers and counteroffers to one another until everyone is happy with the compromise decision package. Sometimes merging the two leading options is the solution, other times collaboratively creating a new option will lead to a satisfactory agreement.
- *Consensus.* A decision is simply accepted as long as no one objects. One person, usually the leader, says, "If no one disagrees, we will_____."
- *Postponing.* Deciding to "not decide," at least for now, is a valid option. Putting off the decision until later might be best if the group does not have the time, people, or expertise to finalize a decision at the moment. In this case, the group must simply decide, "Does this need to be decided now?"

Mike's Best Option. The decision-making method that has been most acceptable in meetings I facilitate is a two-step process. Step one is to strive for consensus, and failing that, step two is to accept a majority vote. The best way I've found to establish this is to obtain buy-in from the group early in the process. I say, "I propose that we work as hard as we can to arrive at a consensus agreement. If we cannot do that, then our fallback decision process will be by majority vote with full and respectful minority reporting. Does that work for you?" Now the ground rules have been established and the group can concentrate on finding solutions.

The next several tips lay out group process tools I use to obtain an optimal decision by the end of a meeting.

Tip 40: Decide by Simple Voting

Need: You simply want to pick the group's favorite and move on to the next agenda item.

Solution: You probably use this easy way to generate a group decision already—voting.

Application: Meeting participants can express a majority opinion by choosing among a set of options. Decide if the voting needs to be anonymous or if it can be transparent, that is, if it will be an advantage to identify which participants voted for particular options. You have several different types of online tools available to implement a fast, efficient voting procedure.

- Utilize the Raise-Hands feature in your meeting software.
- Post a poll, either within your meeting software or via a third-party product like an online survey provider. If you only have one question to discuss and evaluate, a useful asynchronous tool you might want to consider is Tricider (https://www.tricider.com/home). With this free web-based tool, simply post a question before the meeting ("What should we do about ____?"); meeting participants then visit the Tricider website to discuss the pros and cons, and then vote on their favorite.
- Obtain consent—state upfront that the decision will be made as proposed before the meeting and without discussion unless someone has an objection. If there is an objection then the process reverts to negotiation to address the objection in a way that meets everyone's needs and concludes with a consensus or majority vote on the amended proposal.

Tip 41: Decide by Ranking

Need: Sometimes you need to determine how the options stack up when compared to one another. A majority vote is an efficient method for a group to decide, but it is not as thorough or revealing as other methods of group decision making.

Solution: When you need an approach that goes beyond a binary "accept/reject" choice, consider asking the group to rank their choices.

To understand more about meeting participants' thinking, you can modify the voting process and include a poll to compare how the options rank against each other. The result gives greater insight, showing where and to what degree the group preferences converge, rather than simply indicating how divided they are.

Application: You are probably familiar with online tools that allow you to implement this type of group decision method; this is just an additional use-case for your favorite methodologies.

- Use a shared document. Post a spreadsheet on a platform that allows multiple users to enter information at the same time, such as Google Sheets. Label rows with the various options, format columns with the names of the meeting participants, and instruct each person to enter their personal ranking for each option into "their" column. Ideally, use a scoring system that equals the number of options; if there are seven options, then the participants must rank the options from one to seven. Make sure everyone understands the ranking system—it doesn't work if one person assigns "1" to their favorite choice while someone else thinks the highest number gives their favorite choice "more points!" You also can use a rubric such as High, Medium, and Low. Then all you need to do is compute the average ranking in the last column.

- Use a Round Robin roll call of each participant. This is not a good option for a large group as it takes more time, but it can work well with a small, closely-connected team.
- Use a third-party survey tool.

Tip 42: Decide by Scoring

Need: How well do the options meet predetermined evaluation criteria? Sometimes a majority vote or simple ranking doesn't provide the sophisticated understanding that you need—especially if you must justify the meeting outcome to people who did not attend the meeting.

Solution: Consider using an evaluation that scores each option on how well they meet criteria important to the group. For example, if a group must choose between two new software options, they probably need to evaluate each choice based on multiple criteria, such as design, platform effectiveness, ease of use, and price. This evaluation approach provides the ability to score each option, looking at one criterion at a time. After the relative strengths and weaknesses of each option have been quantified, you do a side-by-side comparison, establishing how well the various options fit the needs as defined by the criteria. With this type of chart as a reference point, it is easier to approach the discussion and make an informed decision because there is a clear understanding of where the group thinks each option's strengths and weaknesses lie.

Application: Online implementation options include several familiar and effective tools.

- *Polling Tool.* Use either a numerical scoring rubric or a Likert scale (https://en.wikipedia.org/wiki/Likert_scale).
- *Whiteboard with a Posted Likert or Another Continuous Scale.* This software allows remote users to annotate on the whiteboard when

they score the various options. If you have a lot of options or participants, you will need more than one whiteboard.

- *Shared Spreadsheet.* Using a document-sharing platform, post a shared document such as Google Sheets which allows multiple users to enter information simultaneously. Be aware that this option is more complex to administer because you will need one spreadsheet for each option. Label rows with the criteria and columns with the names of the meeting participants. Instruct the participants to carefully enter their personal scoring for each option based on the various criteria. It is usual to use a Likert scale, which runs from 1 ("This option addresses the criterion very poorly") to 5 ("This option addresses the criterion very well"). Make these spreadsheets available one at a time until all the options are scored. Set up each spreadsheet so it automatically calculates the average score in the final column. Then compile a summary of these last columns for the group to discuss. You can even link this last column from each spreadsheet to a summary spreadsheet, so this compilation can be automatic. This process works well and is very thorough, but the downside is that it takes a fair amount of time to set up and is complex to administer. It's not likely to be something you can build "on the fly" during the meeting where the options are themselves being generated by participants.

Tip 43: Decide by Dot Voting, also Known as Multi-Voting

Need: Perhaps you have too many choices or limited resources. You know you need to winnow a list to a more workable number.

Solution: Dot voting is a fast and easy voting system designed to determine the highest priority items on a list. It allows meeting participants to express a preference for more than one option at the same time, and it tends to balance power because everyone's vote (dot) is equally valued. It creates an immediate sense of engagement and also allows participants to watch the decision process emerge, resulting in a better understanding of how the final choice was made.

Application: The technique is called "Dot Voting" because participants cast their votes in face-to-face meetings by placing a colored, round file label, or sticky dot, next to various items posted on the wall of the room. Each meeting participant receives a fixed number of votes (signified by dots) that they can cast however they want. They can place more than one dot on the same item if they think it is significantly more important or spread their dots across several different items. This allows participants to vote for multiple options and reveals relative priorities rather than declaring a sole winner. Simply counting the dots helps identify the group's preferred options. The items with the most dots rank highest and the ones with the fewest are winnowed out of the ensuing discussion.

Dot-voting is quick and simple in a face-to-face meeting. It also translates well into an online environment.

- Dotstorming.com (https://dotstorming.com/) is an online tool designed specifically for dot voting. Easy, efficient, robust, and free.
- Boardthing.com (https://boardthing.com/), from the same maker as dotstorming.com, allows dot voting on a card-based whiteboard. After registering your account, search the help system for "dot voting" to access a short video explaining how to dot vote on their platform.
- Doodle.com (https://doodle.com/) has a voting module that can be used for simple multi-voting. Be aware there is not a limit to the number of votes each person can cast. That means the meeting participants will need to self-regulate the number of votes they

cast, rather than having the maximum set by you or the meeting administrator.
- Decido (https://mindiply.com/products/decido) is another free group decision-making application for quick and easy dot voting.

Tip 44: Getting out of a "Stuck State"

Need: There comes a time in any meeting when the group gets stuck. This "Stuck State" can be a result of various causes such as conflict, uncertainty, resistance, fear of the unknown, or simple exhaustion. If you can fix it, your group can achieve what Henry Ford meant when he said, "If everyone is moving forward together, then success takes care of itself." So, what can you do about the Stuck State?

Solution: The goal isn't to overcome impasse per se, but to help the meeting participants constructively analyze what problem is embedded in the Stuck State. There often are legitimate reasons for impasse. The meeting leader needs to direct the participants into a discovery process to reveal these reasons, and then help the group co-create a solution.

Application: If you feel you understand what is going on, summarize what's causing the gap and ask the group to suggest ways to close it. Sometimes a simple brainstorm inquiry is all that's needed.

Ask the group to describe the gap with a question like, "Here's what we talked about and what I see as the situation right now. What is the reason we are stuck right now?" Then, follow with an invitation for the group to brainstorm how to close the gap with a question line, "So, the next question is, how can we close this gap? We are going to take the next few minutes to explore our options. I would like you to name some workable solutions that will remove this sticking point and allow us to keep making progress. Who has the first suggestion?"

If you are not sure what is stalling progress, you'll need some intervention strategies.

- *Take a break.* Often, things have a way of looking different when you return.
- *Table the topic.* Ask the group if they agree to set the issue aside temporarily and go on to something else – and come back to the sticky issue later or in a future meeting.
- *Dig out the roots.* Ask the participants to explain their perspectives on why they think there is an impasse. Caution them not to turn this into a pro/con debate and not to criticize others. Sometimes the group needs to focus consciously on the causes of the roadblock and an uncritical listing of all possible causes can lead to a solution.
- *Find personal roadblocks.* Ask each participant to describe any personal difficulties that are holding them back. Hold a judgment-free space in the meeting while this "data" is collected.
- *Look for the big picture.* Try giving a global summary, describing what you see as the sticking point, and then compare it to the overall challenge the group is addressing. Sometimes the issue creating the impasse will dwindle in importance, and won't remain a sticking point when participants shift their perspectives. The group will simply decide to ignore the issue because it does not have much impact on the decision they really need to make.
- *Suggest a trial period or plan.* Sometimes folks will agree to try an interim approach for a short time and then meet again to discuss how it's working.
- *Seek the "why."* Help the participants explore the values behind their resistance. Have the group list criteria for an acceptable outcome. You could say, "Before we focus on the outcome itself, let's

try to define the qualities that a good outcome should have." Clarifying the reasoning that a decision should be based upon can clarify the right choice for removing a sticking point.

- *Use reality-testing.* In a polite way, challenge participants and explicitly confront the consequences of staying mired in a Stuck State. For example, you could ask, "What do you think will happen if this decision remains unmade?" Drawing out the implications of failing to act can re-establish the need to move forward despite any marginal problems that are holding up progress or the fear about making a compromise.

- *Don't fear the last resort.* If all else fails, suggest that failing to decide is, itself, a decision. By insisting on remaining in the Stuck State, they're making a choice that's equivalent to letting someone else make the decision. Suggest that, perhaps, the best course of action is to end the discussion and summarize that status so that the next decision maker has all the information they need to decide. Participants who have invested time and energy in the meeting often do not want to lose the ability to control the outcome—and may suddenly get unstuck.

Groups are capable of great wisdom. Constructively guiding people through their Stuck State is a powerful contribution that a meeting leader can make to harvest that wisdom.

Tip 45: Use Google Forms to Vote on a List of Items

Need: When a group of people is faced with deciding, voting is a common way to assess their collective opinion. The type of vote can vary from single choice (winner-take-all) to negative voting (eliminates the weakest options) to multi-voting (pares down a variety of options into a manageable shortlist). No matter which type of decision you are looking for, the votes must be collected somehow. Fortunately, there are many web-based options available. Most meeting platforms have a voting option, but sometimes it is more efficient to have the voting occur asynchronously—after the meeting, so people have a chance to ruminate, or between meetings, so they come prepared to discuss how to implement the decision.

Solution: Google Forms is free web-based survey software that enables you to collect information from users easily, using a personalized survey or quiz connected to a spreadsheet. This service supports multiple people participating in the survey at the same time. You can add standard question types, drag-and-drop questions in any order you choose, and customize the form with simple photo or color themes. You can review the gathered responses directly in Forms, or save them using the pre-populated, connected Google Sheets spreadsheet. It's easy to use and one of the simplest ways to collect data.

Google Forms allows a group of people to simultaneously give their input and view the results in real time. When complete, these results can be saved or exported for use in other documents and spreadsheets. I have had great success using Google Docs and Google Forms for brainstorming.

Application: Perhaps you see the value in the Google Forms/Google Docs connection but want a quick lesson on using Google Forms. If so, head on over to these how-to videos.

https://www.youtube.com/watch?v=W7wOQaGbf-A - Published by https://AnsonAlex.com.

https://youtu.be/NoDdww9MoNs - Published by https://dottotech.com

When you need to compile group opinions outside of the actual meetings, a Google Form is your best friend. To see how this works, view the sample survey I created for you at http://tinyurl.com/Favorite MarxBro and vote for your favorite Marx Brother!

References

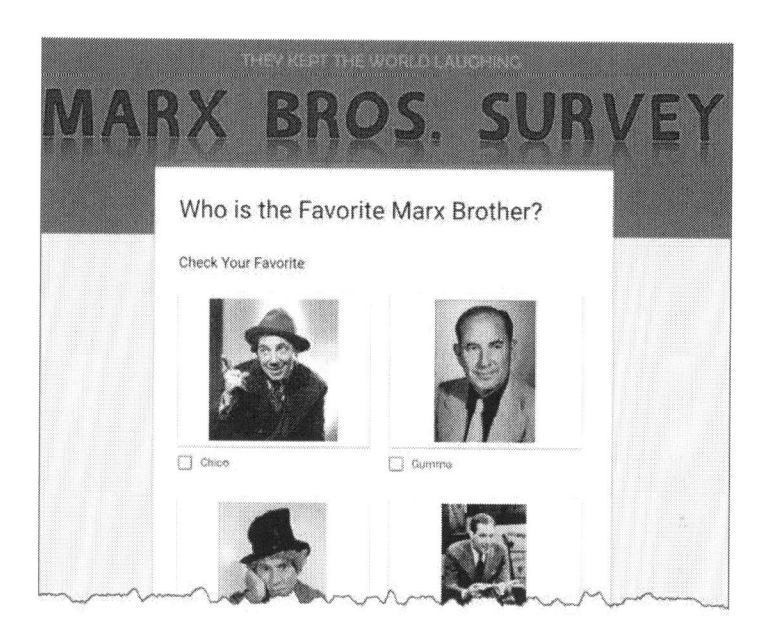

Tip 46: If You Can't Prevent a Group from Wordsmithing, Provide Good Orienteering by Using Line Numbers

Need: Does this situation sound familiar? You are trying to lead a meeting toward conclusion but you can't prevent the group from going through a long document line by line before they'll agree to final edits. Ugh! They're wordsmithing again!

One of the most difficult challenges with group editing, especially if the document is large, is literally getting everyone on the same page... not to mention on the same line... in order to discuss the same item.

Solution: Provide precise orientation for participants using line numbering and page numbers. Fortunately, most word processing software programs can add line numbers on each page. With that solution, you are all set to issue your orientation instructions.

Application: By adding line numbers you will never have to say this again: "Turn to Section 1.10.32 and find the paragraph that starts with

'But I must explain....' Now, look at the second sentence in that paragraph which begins with, 'No one rejects...'"

With line numbers, orientation is simple: "Turn to page 43, line 26." Which option would you prefer to use?

Add line numbers, then remove them when the editing is complete.

Tip 47: Dealing with the Person Who is Reluctant to Agree

Need: Every meeting leader must deal with objectors—you know, those people who are stubbornly withholding their support for an agreement that the rest of the group is ready to endorse. When that happens, the discussion focuses on one subject: "What's wrong with this decision?" Usually, the objector focuses on what they dislike about the proposal, not what they actually want or prefer. Their comments commonly begin with phrases like, "I don't think this will work because...," "I don't like this idea because...," or "I can't support this because...." Then, they list all their objections. Worse, they rarely offer solutions to the problems they have raised. Their implicit message is, "Here is my problem—I want you to fix it for me."

Solution: Use a Turn-Around Question.

Application: Ask the objector to solve his/her own problem but, importantly, do so with a very carefully worded Turn-Around Question.

"Thanks for sharing your concerns. What is a solution that will work for you *and* work for everyone else at the same time? In other words, what is a suggestion that will work for everyone?"

A Turn-Around Question accomplishes two things. The first part of the question, "What is a solution that will work for you ... " makes the objector accountable for finding the solution, rather than pushing that responsibility onto the other people in the meeting. The second part of the question, "... *and* work for everyone else at the same time?" prompts the objector to acknowledge and accept the needs of the other group members. Asking this two-part question shifts the conversation from being about *me* and *my* needs to a dialog about *our* needs—in other words, a collaborative solution.

Be sure to reword the Turn-Around Question to fit the context of your interaction with the objector as well as your communication style and preferences. Be artful and diplomatic, but don't hesitate to ask this challenging question. Encourage the objector to own the responsibility to solve his/her own problem and honor the social contract he/she has with the other people in the room to meet their needs at the same time.

Tip 48: Test for Agreement—Have Your Toolbox Ready

Need: In a face-to-face meeting it is easy to ask, "Are we in agreement?" and then look around the room for acknowledgment. You'll see people nodding their heads, waving their hands, and giving a thumbs up. You get an answer without anyone saying a word. But online meetings are inherently awkward because you cannot see the non-verbal behavior of participants.

Solution: In an online meeting, checking for understanding and acknowledgment requires a more-structured process.

Application: Make sure your toolbox contains several methods to test for agreement. You'll develop your own, but you can start with some common strategies.

- *Silence Voting.* Restate the decision you think the group just made, then tell everyone you are using a silence-means-agreement vote for this item. You might say, "If you agree with the proposal I just summarized, all you need to do is remain silent for the next few moments. If you have a concern or a gut feeling that says we have not yet come to an agreement, we will give you a chance to explain it and you can ask for reconsideration. Otherwise, silence means we have an agreement." Then be quiet for 10-20 seconds.
- *Hand Raise—Positive Voting.* If your meeting software has the Raise Hand feature, use that tool for a direct vote from the partic-

ipants who agree. Restate the decision you think the group just made, then invite the response. Simply say, "If you agree, please raise your hand now." Count the number of raised hands and compare that with the total number of people in the meeting. If there are *any* objectors, follow up with a second round of voting. Reset the hand-raise voting results, then say: "If you were unable to vote to agree, raise your hand this time if your concern is great enough that you would like us to talk about it and reconsider the decision." Then tackle the objections, perhaps using a Turn-Around Question (see Tip 47).

- *Hand Raise—Disagreement Check*. This is the same process as Silence Voting, except it uses the Raise Hand tool to identify if anyone has a concern that is so large that they would like to put the brakes on the decision process and discuss their concerns. People who agree with the decision should leave their virtual hand down.
- *Three-Number Rating*, also known as *Virtual Thumb Voting*. In a face-to-face meeting, an effective tool for testing for agreement is thumb voting. You re-state the decision that you think the group is making, then ask participants to vote with their thumbs:
    o Thumb Up means, "I support this proposal."
    o Thumb Sideways means, "I'll go along with the proposal."
    o Thumb Down means, "I do not support this proposal and wish to talk more about it."

In an online meeting, however, you can't see any thumbs (unless you are using webcams for each person in the audience). Instead, ask people to 'vote' in the chatbox using the scoring rule, 1 means Thumb Up, 2 means Thumb Sideways, and 3 means Thumb Down.

- *Segue Out to a Polling Service*. If your meeting software allows polling and you have the ability to create an instant poll as the meeting progresses, do it. This is a good task for your online meeting assistant. As an alternative, have participants log into a third-party polling service such as the polling feature in Google Drive. Bear in mind that this is difficult to do on the fly, so this technique may be more effective as an asynchronous activity between online meetings. I once set up this type of poll over a meal break. When we adjourned for a long lunch, my assistant and I built a quick poll and sent the participants an email with a link to the poll. They were required to complete the poll before we resumed after the lunch break. We began the afternoon session with a review of the poll results, then tweaked the group's recommendation to finalize it. It was definitely faster than trying to discuss everything in real time or holding a second meeting on another day. It was quite a bit of rushed work, but worth it!

- *Parking Lot.* This common tool used in face-to-face meetings is just as useful for online meetings. When something comes up that's not relevant to the discussion or can be safely deferred, "park" it in another section of the meeting notes. This set of notes is usually labeled "Parking Lot," but I have noticed increasing resistance to that term. Some meeting participants interpret the Parking Lot as a convenient way for the leader to kill their idea or concern. I have started using substitute terms for labeling these notes, like "Issues for Next Time," "NFN (Not for Now)," "Waiting Room," and "Follow-Up List." I have not yet found a perfect alternative term, so be creative if you encounter criticism when using the term "Parking Lot." Regardless of how it's named, do make this list visible online by creating a separate note sheet devoted to it. This allows the group to stay focused while also reassuring participants with an off-topic idea that they were heard and their concerns acknowledged. If time permits, near the end of the meeting you can visit the Parking Lot and have participants make some decisions about how to handle the items on that list.

AFTER THE MEETING TIPS:
WHEN THE MEETING IS OVER, IT'S NOT OVER

Don't assume that ideas discussed during a meeting will be put into action immediately or even remembered. It does not matter how productive the meeting was if the follow-up flops. Typically, participants immediately run to another meeting or rush off to deal with other priorities as their attention shifts to a new set of issues. Sometimes people leave a meeting without clarity about what was agreed. Good online meetings make decisions. Great online meetings make sure it is clear how these decisions will be implemented.

Tip 49: Write it Down

Need: The group already decided on the issue, right? Surely, everyone will remember, right? Think again. Too often, what's not written down gets lost.

Solution: Most of the time, creating a meeting record is not hard. But there is a sliding scale for how formal the meeting record should be. If you are leading a formal meeting of record, like a public hearing or contract negotiation, then pull out the stops and create a detailed log of all proceedings. Most of the time, however, our online meetings do not carry that burden. We are usually hosting working meetings, and these do not need that level of formality. Let's look at how to capture the outcome of a typical working meeting.

Application: For work meetings, it is important to capture the essence of the meeting, not "he said/she said" dialogues. Start by documenting the key details:

- *decisions made*
- *reasons for the decisions*
- *planned next steps*
- *identification and tracking of action items*
- *assignments*

As the meeting leader, make the following decisions as you plan the meeting:

1. *Recruiting a notetaker.* It is usually best to find someone who can show initiative, has good listening skills, can correctly assimilate meaning from the dialog, and has the needed note-taking skills.

After the Meeting Tips

Meet with the notetaker before the meeting to review the agenda and talk over the purpose of each agenda item. Strive to create a team relationship, not just an assignment to the notetaker. A good notetaker is a solid team player and a quick thinker, not just a scribe typing into a computer.

2. Notetaking at the meeting. Decide what kind of record each agenda item will generate. Communicate this expectation to your note-taking teammate. If you need a bullet list for an agenda item, tell your notetaker. If you need a pros/cons narrative for an agenda item, tell your notetaker. You get the idea—coach your notetaker so they know what to expect from each agenda item.
3. Writing after the meeting. Decide who will turn the meeting notes into the draft version of the meeting record, how they'll do it, and how quickly. Also, decide what type of editing and approval process will be necessary to generate the final document. Pin down who will be responsible for document creation and what approval process will be followed.
4. Distributing the meeting record. To whom? How? When? Who will do this?
5. Filing or storing. Decide how the final document will be archived if any backup copies are required, and who will ensure this is done.

Tip 50: When the Meeting is Over, You Still Have Work to Do

Need: There usually are unaddressed details that remain after a meeting ends. And, because a meeting is a social process, participants will respond to authentic appreciation.

Solution: Create a list of work tasks after the meeting to close the loop on undone details. To show your participants respect, give them a warm closing message, congratulating them on their accomplishments and expressing your appreciation for their hard work.

Application: Add these three after-meeting tasks to your checklist of planning tasks.

1. Transfer Meeting Files. Be sure to prepare and transfer copies of these items:
   - the inputs to your meeting (slides, background documents, etc.)
   - the outcomes of your meeting (a meeting report, decision packet, list of conclusions, written agreement, etc.)
   - the next steps (tasks, assignments, future schedule implications, etc.)
2. Send out final work assignments. If there were details not completed by the end of the meeting, now is the time to document them and issue any assignments to make sure they get done. If there is unfinished business, send that as a separate communication, perhaps titled something clever like, "Unfinished Business from Our Meeting" or "Assignments from Our Meeting."
3. Humans like receiving acknowledgment for their work and participation in a team. As the meeting leader, consider sending one or more of the following messages after the meeting so your participants know they are valued.

- Send a follow-up note of thanks—we all like to receive some version of "Thanks, you did great work."
- Follow up with feedback indicating how their contribution was used or implemented.
- Give team members a report describing their colleagues' success with follow-up tasks.

After the Meeting Tips

- Send a follow-up question asking for their advice on a spin-off issue from your meeting.
- Send meeting minutes on time and in a useful format such as an infographic, especially if participants can turn around and use it to inform others about the meeting outcome.
- Write and share personal notes and reflections about the outcomes of the meeting. This is probably better if it is less formal, such as a greeting card since it is your personal message.
- If the group is new, provide a contact list of participants and areas of expertise.
- Celebrate achievements! How about having the big boss send an appreciation to participants?

CONTINUOUS SELF-IMPROVEMENT: SLOW IMPROVEMENT IS NOT BAD, STANDING STILL IS BAD

Get a little bit better with every meeting. Successfully adding online meeting leadership to your resumé is not about getting the current meeting right. It is about incremental improvement. A good mantra is, "No meeting is perfect; there's always room to improve." Getting better with each event will make your job easier and more pleasant, you'll be saving time and money by avoiding bad meetings, and you'll be getting far better value out of your meetings as you continuously learn how to transform meetings where only talking occurs into meetings that inspire action.

Tip 51: Seek Balanced Coaching for Continuous Improvement

Need: Silence is not a good teacher. It is hard to improve without feedback.

Solution: Create an explicit way to get feedback about your online meetings. Feedback is the cheapest, most powerful, yet most under-used management tool that meeting leaders can have in their toolbox. It serves as a guide for continuous improvement. And it can be both motivating and energizing.

Application: Strength-based coaching seeks to create a person's best performance by focusing on strengths. Strength-based coaching considers the question, "What will happen when we think about what is right with people rather than focusing on what is wrong with them?" (Donald O. Clifton, *Soar With Your Strengths*, Dell Publishing). As your coach, if I only said critical things it would be easy for you to interpret my messages as saying that your performance is always sub-par. Proponents of strength-based coaching say that a quicker road to higher performance is to focus on strengths and strive to make you better in these dimensions. Why? Because you get higher performance levels by building on what you are already good at, not by only looking at ways to remediate deficits. In short, it is easier and quicker to build on excellence because we are tapping into your existing assets and shifting the internal dialogue from "I can't" to "I can do more."

But there is other research that throws some controversy around this conclusion. This alternative view is that there is a place for negative feedback as part of performance improvement. Furthermore, high-performing leaders tend to get better by developing new strengths and focusing on carefully chosen deficits, as well as enhancing existing strengths (Tomas Chamorro-Premuzic, Harvard Business Review, January 4, 2016).

So, what should you do when you are ready to seek feedback on your performance as a leader of online meetings? I am firmly in the camp that believes negative feedback coaching is defeating. At the same time, I can see the logic that avoiding deficit correction is, basically, ignoring problems. For me, the solution is to seek balanced coaching which focuses on three key factors: current strengths to build upon, new strengths that will improve effectiveness, and reducing deficits where a correction will generate better outcomes. In highly sophisticated mathematical terms,

$$\text{PERFORMANCE IMPROVEMENT} = \text{EXISTING STUFF TO KEEP DOING} + \text{NEW STUFF TO START DOING} + \text{SOME STUFF TO WORK ON}$$

The best experience I ever had with this approach was with master facilitator Leska Fore. I once facilitated a meeting where she was present. I asked her to watch me and give input, and fortunately for me, she said, "Yes." Leska used the following framework to document her observations on specific aspects of my facilitation skills, where she could see improvement opportunities. Hands down, this was the best coaching I ever received.

From time to time, consider asking a trusted colleague who knows your work to observe one of your online meetings and offer this kind of balanced feedback.

[Handwritten feedback notes table, annotated with "Feedback Codes" (upper left: WD = Well Done, OFI = Opportunity for Improvement) and "Three Evaluation Factors" pointing to the column headings.]

Code	OBSERVATION	IMPACT	SUGGESTION
WD	Invite people to agree or propose an action =	members learn difference B/N stray comments & comments that move to action.	
OFI	Ask for head nods for agreement & adoption.	Difficult to see if all are ok.	use hands or cards? Forces everyone to participate.
WD	Discussion is guided & structured by MF	I know where we are	
WD	Ask members to turn comments into proposals.	Pushes each member to own & decide (DISCERN?) what is important; feeling of completion and decision.	
WD	Ask NH what she wants from the group structure	Gives members a job besides just listening.	
WD	Small groups & inspired energetic engagement	I feel optimistic about group's commitment	
OFI	Some people impatient with lack of content in discussion, too much process?	more small group work, less big group	
WD	MF asked for feedback from group.	I trust you to facilitate & listen.	

Copy of feedback notes from one of the author's facilitations. Note the feedback codes in the upper left corner and how that was used with the three evaluation factors in the heading of this table. Used with permission from Leska Fore.

Tip 52: Form a Mastermind Group

Need: "'You are the average of the five people you spend the most time with'" (unknown). If you do not have five (or so) like-minded and trusted colleagues who can give you advice, read on.

Solution: Form a mastermind group. A mastermind group consists of a few people who meet several times each year with the intention of accelerating one another's personal development. It's a reciprocal relationship around a topic that meets all group members' needs. Your topic, I hope, would be *Mastering Online Meetings*!

Application: Keys for the success of a mastermind group are that all members truly care about everyone else's success, the members face challenges that are similar enough that everyone has an interest in their solution, and everyone actively participates.

Mastermind discussions should resist the urge to be about making judgments and, instead, be about exploration that leads to brainstorming new possibilities. They set up accountability structures to keep the person receiving advice focused and on track. In this way you create a community of supportive colleagues who learn, problem solve, and move forward together. For an individual member, being part of a mastermind group is like having a supportive and objective board of directors, a coaching team, and a peer advisory group all rolled into one.

What is a good size for the mastermind group? Keep it small, between four and eight people. With fewer than four, the energy and synergy can swiftly drop. But with more than eight members, you will probably run out of time in your meetings. If this is a new concept for you, start small and slowly build up to a larger group.

Can a mastermind group function with only two people? Yes. In this model, you team up with a like-minded colleague for regular coaching and support. As you would with a larger group, decide on a format and timing that works for you.

If you're sold on the concept and just need to learn how to manage such a group, consider these questions:

- How much time is available for each meeting? Remember, everyone struggles with the problem of having too much to do and not enough time. Allocate enough time for fruitful conversations but not so much that people can't afford to be away from their already-busy lives.

- Meet on a regular schedule. Because improving our skills is valuable, scheduling consistent mastermind sessions becomes an investment of time that yields high-value returns.

- How much time should each member have in the spotlight to talk about their problem, challenge or decision need? Every individual should reap benefits (receive input from the other members) at every meeting, so work out a solution that gives adequate attention to each person. Members will need time to verbalize their situations before masterminding can begin in earnest. There also needs to be a conversation to explore what happened or what the member currently desires. Follow that up with a "What's next?" conversation. If you're not sure, begin by allocating 30 minutes for each person and assess how that works for your mastermind group's unique dynamics. Be aware that each person must own the responsibility to be clear and succinct, so the meeting does not stall on one person's issues.

Do you need a facilitator? Yes. Otherwise, conversations may wander. Share facilitator duties. Task the facilitator with ensuring that everyone has spotlight time, the conversations are deep and balanced, and all agenda items are covered. The facilitator's job description consists of managing time and moderating a rich conversation that produces a concrete outcome for each individual.

Do you need a meeting agenda? Yes. A set agenda usually works well. As your mastermind evolves, you'll come up with your own agenda and the right questions to answer; but if you don't know where to begin, here is a sample agenda for a round-robin conversation.

- Designated Individual Conversations (focus on one person at a time). Call-and-response feedback discussion from each person who wants to explore a need they have such as the following:
    - "A challenge I encountered was _____."
    - "What I need from you today is _____."
    - "Help me brainstorm—what can be done about _____?"
    - "I'm making a commitment to try _____ next."
- Conclude the agenda with a positive closing, conversation, or activity.

Always remember what a mastermind group is NOT.

- It's not a class. The focus is on brainstorming and accountability support among the group members on their specific challenges.
- It's not a networking group. You are not attending the mastermind meeting to "work the room." While you may share leads and resources with each other, this is not the purpose of mastermind meetings.
- It's not counseling. The goal isn't therapy. It is to gently explore each member's needs through debriefing, active listening, and asking questions (especially open-ended questions).
- Mastermind conversations avoid judgment and emphasize exploration.

CONCLUSION: A PERSON'S MOST IMPORTANT ACHIEVEMENT IS THEIR NEXT ONE

If something you try in your online meetings does not work out the way you intended, don't beat yourself up. It's easy to sink into a motivation trough. It's normal, so expect it. Resist the temptation to evaluate yourself on a single experience. Reframe the definition of success as engaging in life-long learning and improvement.

I once asked Andrea Mead Lawrence, an Olympic ski champion with multiple gold medals, about her many successes. She said, "Mike, a person's most important achievement is their next one. Each race, no matter the outcome, is practice for the next one."

Also, consider what other thoughtful people had to say about "learning your way" to success.

"99 percent of success is built on failure." Charles Kettering (American inventor, engineer, businessman, and the holder of 186 patents)

"Success is not final, failure is not fatal; it is the courage to continue that counts." Winston Churchill (Prime Minister of the United Kingdom during World War II)

"Of course, there is no chance of success, if you didn't try." Vineet Raj Kapoor (author, lyricist, poet, game designer, and academic)

"Continuous improvement is better than delayed perfection." Mark Twain

In any improvement process, failure precedes success. Instead of expecting to get it right every time you run an online meeting, you are simply looking for continuous improvement. I've tried to present tips you can use to improve your online meetings. Apply these tips and see what happens. Then, continue to use the tips that work, adapt the tips that can be improved for your specific situation, and pass over any tips that are not right for you. The goal is for you to make them your own, in order to get a little bit better each time you run an online meeting.

Consider adopting the Rule of Three. If you try something once and it does not work for you, remember that innovation typically requires three tries to get it right. By the third time you use one of the tips, you will see if you can make that tip produce your desired outcome. If a tip just does not work, you will learn that as well, and can freely abandon it.

TIP of the WEEK Finally, improvement comes one tip at a time. Set aside time each week to read a tip and consider how you can use it or how you can adapt it to make your next online meeting more productive, stress free, and enjoyable.

We are all works in progress. Becoming frustrated is normal. Minimize how much time you spend in a motivation trough. Shake it off by doing what Andrea Mead Lawrence did to make herself an Olympic champion—*think forward*. Thinking backward and criticizing yourself is not the way to design the future. Instead, learn from your experiences and make them constructive by thinking over the lessons you've learned, then thinking forward about improvements you want to carry into your next challenge.

Never neglect the opportunity to improve. Every one of us is a work in progress—embrace the process!

Printed in Great Britain
by Amazon